SOCIAL SECURITY OF LABOUR IN INDIA AND ECONOMIC REFORMS

SOCIAL SECURITY OF LABOUR IN INDIA AND ECONOMIC REFORMS

Edited By
K.M. NAIDU
Dept. of Economics
Sri Venkateswara University
Tirupati (A.P.)

SERIALS PUBLICATIONS
NEW DELHI

SOCIAL SECURITY OF LABOUR IN INDIA AND ECONOMIC REFORMS

ISBN: 81-86771-11-5
Price : Rs. 395

Published by: **SERIALS PUBLICATIONS**
4, B.S.S. Hall, Khyber Pass Market,
Civil Lines, Delhi—110054 (India)
Phone: 91-11-3811659
Fax: 91-11-3812678
Email: serials @satyam.net.in
Branch Office: 4830/24, Ansari Road, Darya Ganj,
New Delhi—110002 (India)
Phone: 0091-11-3245225

Typesetting by: **Sarita Enterprises,** Ghaziabad

Dedicated to

KARL MARX

the World Great Genius

CONTENTS

List of Contributors viii
Foreward x
Introduction xii
Contributors' Articles xviii
1. Economic Reforms and Social Security of Labour in India 1
2. Impact of Social Security Initiatives in Unorganised Sector: The Case of Women Beedi Workers in Rural Areas of Tamil Nadu 27
3. Social Security for the Workers in the Informal Construction Sector 53
4. Social Security for Workers in the Unorganised Sector 63
5. Social Security for Rural Labour: Existing Provisions and Institutional Arrangement 79
6. Social Security for Rural Labour in India 105
7. Social Security for Women Workers in India 120

CONTRIBUTORS	TITLE OF THE ARTICLE
1. **K. Munirathna Naidu,** UGC Emeritus Fellow Department of Economics, Sri Venkatesawara University, Tirupati—517 502, Andhra Pradesh.	Economic Reforms and Social Security of Labour in India.
2. **K. Srinivasulu Naidu,** Department of Economics, Sri Venkateswara University, Tirupati—517 502, A.P.	- do -
3. **Mrs. P. Manjushree Naidu** Ph.D., Research Scholar, Department of Economics, Sri Venkateswara University, Tirupati—517 502, A.P.	- do -
4. **Velayutham Saravanan,** Project Associate, Madras Institute of Development Studies, Adyar, Chennai—600 020 Tamil Nadu.	Impact of Social Security initiatives in unorganised sector: The Case of Women Beedi workers in Rural Areas of Tamil Nadu.
5. **B. Vanitha,** Reader in Economics, PSG College of Arts & Sciences, Coimbator—641 014, Tamil Nadu.	Social Security for the workers in the informal construction Sector.
6. **Jayashree Dam P. Choudhary,** Research Scholar, Department of Commerce, Guwahati University, Guwahati—14, Assam.	Social Security for workers in the Unorganised Sector.

CONTRIBUTORS	TITLE OF THE ARTICLE
7. **S.P. Singh,** Associate Professor, Department of Humanities & Social Science Indian Institute of Technology, Roorkee.	Social Security for Rural Labour: Existing Provisions and Institutional Arrangement.
8. **Vipla Chopra,** Reader in Economics, Punjab University, Patiala Punjab.	Social Security for Rural Labour in India.
9. **G. Subbayamma,** Reader in School of Management Studies, Indira Gandhi National Open University, New Delhi.	Social Security for Women Workers in India.
10. **S. Vijaya Kumar,** Fellow of RBI Chair, Council for Social Development, Southern Regional Office, Hyderabad.	- do -

FOREWARD

India began an enthusiastic phase of economic reforms since 1991. The explicit idea of reforms was mainly to bring down public involvement in many production and distribution mechanisms whose performance can be accelerated and turned profitable by private sector. Unexpectedly this process affected the genuine performance of the public action in implementing social sector and the related poverty alleviation programmes. No doubt private participation improves the quality of service but at the same time becomes expensive which may be beyond the capacity of major portion of the people. Hence the state intervention is necessary to fulfill its constitutional obligation of providing basic services to people at the cost of government. India's place in social sector set up is very low and if people are left on their own, they cannot improve the position and hence public support is quite essential.

It is pertinent to remember here the financial position of State, both central and State Governments. The reforms in particular impose burden on the State finances in two ways. (1) The tax GDP ratios are not increasing in tune with increases of GDP; there is very often shortfall compared to targeted collections. (2) However, rise in GDP growth requires (mostly by way of demand) reallocation of public funds more to industry, infrastructure and service sectors compared to social sectors, poverty alleviation programmes, rural development and primary sectors. In a sense, the latter are usually the victims and secure lower allocation at the hands of the government when it is under financial strain.

The government through budget allocation, performs a

facilitator role by setting apart amounts to priority sectors with a view to promote efficiency in growth, sustainability and equity in development. This instrument of budget has to be wielded effectively to face emerging issues and challenges. It has to show both flexibility and dynamism to meet the basic demands of education, health, and other activities that contribute to the higher standard of life of common people. In a sense, more budgetary allocations are imperative to galvanise rural and agricultural economy which help improve levels in social sector and reduce poverty as 65% of people live in rural India where illiteracy, ill health and poverty are at higher levels and hence the need for higher spending on social sector to boost the general demand for achieving higher economic growth of 8 to 10% in India.

The contributors of this volume have done a good job of analysing the challenges faced by lower allocations to social sector affecting lobour and their productivity and gave relevant suggestions to improve the neglected dimension of social security of labour. Both the Centre and State government have to play an effective, catalytic role to boost the living conditions of organised and unorganised labour. It is to be hoped that the Tenth Five Year Plan in operation since 1st April 2002 and the subsequent plans would provide more amounts to widen the scope of social security benefits to labour in the interest of higher growth of economy where labour's role is abundantly important as that of other factors of production.

August 1, 2002 **K.M. Naidu**

INTRODUCTION: NEED FOR A GENUINE NATIONAL SOCIAL SECURITY POLICY

As in the case of other ideas, social security concept has been down loaded on to the developing economies. United Kingdom initiated social security measures for labour after industrial revolution by covering the risks of life from cradle to grave. It is the Beveredige report submitted in 1942 stand like torch bearer for the countries who want to introduce social security measures. The changes that take place in society have their reflection in policies adopted for providing security to labour. There is an evolution of definition on social security from ILO (1980s) to UNDP (1994) stressing on different aspects. The liberalisation and globalisation introduced in many developing countries in the recent past since 1980s have their own impact. In a sense the provision of social security by governments is slowly evolving, sometimes benefiting the workers substantially and many times touching them only pheripherally.

The social security has been clearly explained in 1990 by E. Ahmed and Jean Dreze. It relates to the direct role that public (government) action can play in reducing human deprivation and eliminating vulnerability in a developing country. The emphasis is on the use of means in terms of publication to follow some specific objectives like reduction of deprivation and vulnerability. The justification for this emphasis emnates from the fact that many developing countries have higher percentage of unorganised/informal sectors and these workers do not have access to the benefits of traditional sociál security schemes. Even the benefits provided to the workers in organised sector is far from satisfactory and are not equal to the needs and normal requirements of this class of workers.

Whether Human Development preceeds real implementation of social security schemes or vice-verse is not easy to resolve as it depends upon capacity of the country and the attitude of the people. No doubt social security measures protect the workers from relapsing into below minimum standard of living particularly at the time of economic crises and unforeseen contingencies. In countries like India social security cannot be limited to social risk management, nor equated with human development. Hence the role of State and its intervention emerges as a primary task.

Position in India

In India social security programmes are of two types: (1) protective social security measures like medical care, benefits of sickness, maternity, old age etc. This relates mostly to workers in organised sector, (2) promotional security covering the workers in unorganised sector. This refers to self employment, wage employment and provision of basic needs like food, health and education. Due to many problems and loopholes the benefits from these measures reach only a small percentage of the people. To set right tis lacunae it is suggested to extend the area of social security to different vulnerable groups within the unorganised sector.

Globalisation laid bare the neglected aspects of social security in India. Along with liberalisation and privatisation, Globalisation showed its neutrality in distributing its impact unless positive intervention by government made efforts to set right the ill effects. Globalisation led to jobless growth along with the removal of labour through the instrument of hire and fire used indiscriminately by the entrepreneurs and owners of factories. This led to rise in poverty, deprivation vulnerability and marginalisation of labour. In the Indian case the problem became surprisingly serious. The government of India made the employers to follow committedly social security protection for those employed by them. But the reality is that the workers in the organised sector began to decline from 13 to 10% in the past decade and to 7% in 2002. It means the structural adjustment programme assiduously followed by government since June 1990 (as a second item of economic reforms) led to more insecurity amongst the workers as the share of unorganised sector workers rose. The special schemes—like pension to agricultural workers and measures by individual states like Tamil Nadu and Maharashtra—have been neglected. Andhra Pradesh has also implemented poverty reduction initiation project (Velugu Scheme) with the aid (grant) from World Bank to the extent of Rs. 2450 crores to protect the rural poor labour (Upliftment to 6.20 lakhs BPL families) from deprivation and vulnerability (The Hindu dt. 18-5-2002, p. 1 and June 5, 2002, p. 3). The scheme aimed at alleviating poverty in 500 mandals in 16 districts and would be extended to the entire State.

Hence there is every need for initiatives at the country level by central government to start comprehensive social policy covering all sections and sectors of labour. The contributors in the volume analysed the impact of social security policy implemented in several parts of India and revealed many inadequacies of the implementation programmes and suggested a wholesome national policy related to social security of labour. The indepth studies made focused on some sectors and in some parts of the country (health, education, awareness etc.). The main objective of the volume is to present an overview of social security provided in India, to point out some of the drawbacks of the policies implemented by government and to suggest practical methods to overcome them. In June 2002, National Labour Commission submitted its report to government of India incorporating wide ranging recommendations touching upon social security of labour treating it as a National concern and obligations.

The book adds further knowledge to arrive at a comprehensive social security policy by government in the context of fear of neglect of labour by government due to market-led growth policies followed in the unavoidable attractive globalisation era thrust on government because world Trade Organisation policies approved by government of India. Competition is inevitable and survival is also inevitable, more so for the labour. The government of India and State governments would initiate, it is hoped, sector specific and area relevant programmes to uplift the poor labour from venerability, deprivation and maginalisation as their role is significant in the globalisation process of the economy. Discontentment, hunger, poverty, illiteracy and low levels of living any where found in the country and neglected for long will lead to violence and indiscipline which will postpone development for several decades throwing India to low levels of development index in the global scenario. The book has reflected on the facts relating to the timely topic of social security of labour in India, gave several significant suggestions to help labour, through government intervention, overcome deprivating, vulnerability and marginalisation so as to make them live a comparatively better life and help in the process of growth of the economy to make India a model nation and highly developed country in the world by the end of tenth Five Year Plan. Nationalise first the rural sector and then globalise rural sector as well as social security sector.

After the award of Nobel prize in Economics to Prof. Amartya Kumar Sen for his seminal contribution to Welfare Economics with its implications on individual empowerment, entitlement, freedom, social security etc. the significance of issues relating to social security of labour became relevant and topical. His emphasis on government intervention in the event of market failures and the consequent ill-effects particularly on vulnerable groups like labour acquired urgent focus and the researchers began to divert their attention on the efforts made by government to increase social welfare facilities to labour. The present volume also adds to the existing research knowledge on the contributions made by Central and State governments to improve labour welfare through higher allocations to social security programmes. In India expenditure set aside gains relevante as the potential beneficiaries of social security measures, particularly basic needs, often impinges on less articulate and disadvanted (less powerful) groups.

The contributors in the volume analysed critically on many aspects like social security policies, food, nutrition, health and housing, education, employment, vulnerable groups, experience of States, both failures and success, mostly depending upon basic data and at times field survey material to arrive at conclusions relevant to the objectives kept in view by the individual contributor. Overall conclusion is that the existing social security benefits made available to labour is quite inadequate and hence improved substantially in future-through adequate provision of money is necessary as well as its efficient spending so as to make the benefits reach the vulnerable and deprived sections in a judicious way for allowing them live a higher standard of living.

Future Outlook

Social security system has to be redesigned by giving wholesome approach with the main aim of meeting the basic needs of the poor and marginal sections. The volume pointed to the inadequacies of policies, both in money and implementation aspects. The expenditures made to social sector conveniently left out 93% of the labour. The globalisation policies followed by India since 1990s under scores the need for a comprehensive social security policies for a large section of the society particularly unorganised labour.

The book unveils the nature of future action to be adopted by policy makers and the government towards social security of labour. Even in the case of organised sector, the workers are facing removal from employment (through VRS), casualisation, retrenchment, displacement etc from which the workers are to be protected through suitable labour friendly policies.

All the unorganised work force face insecure future and hence lack the minimum needs in terms of health, housing, education, employment, food and nutrition. They are suffering from the vicious circle of lack of employment, low levels of living and insecure future. Hence these sections urgently require a comprehensive protective policy. Though the researchers emphasize the need for social security of neglected workers, yet social security has not acquired the required attention from government and the development policy of India. It becomes imperative that the stake holders build up sufficient political pressure to achieve their goal. In this effort the researchers would definitely extend their helping hand both at the level of government and policy making and implementation.

August 1, 2002 **K.M. Naidu**

CONTRIBUTORS' ARTICLES

Prof. K.M. Naidu and others in their seminal paper dealt extensively on the macro aspects of social security of labour in India. The idea of the authors is to examine whether economic reforms helped increase social security benefits to workers; if so, to what extent. They have answered several questions relating to social security system implemented for labour in India. Their view is that the interest in this subject of social security gained much significance after the award of Noble prize in Economics to Prof. Amartya Kumar Sen in 1998 for his outstanding contributions in the field of Welfare Economics.

The second section deals with definition of social security from Beveridge Committee Report (1942) to ILO (1992) and to UNDP in 1994. Nearly five issues identified by the authors are low employment growth with high GDP growth, casualisation and marginalisation of workers, jobless growth neutralised by self employment process, the sufferings of poor workers and the quality of employment.

In section III growth promoting policies were analysed. Two approaches were identified-promotion of economic growth to raise incomes and was called as growth mediated security and support led security. For organised workers government followed growth mediated security and (7% of total workers as on March 2002) provided them benefits like provident fund, gratuity, dividends etc. But in the case of unorganised workers, government adopted both growth promoting and support led policies. No doubt it is near impossible to cover with social security benefits for all the poor workers in India (both large and massive).

Growth promoting policies aimed at increasing employment opportunities. These are likely to improve social and economic security for the unorganised workers. Such a policy may bring about structural changes through growth of the economy. In this type of policy, government role is limited only as a facilitator for private investment and skill improvement. The authors also discussed in this sub-title macro strategies for growth of agriculture in rainfed areas in particular where there is possibility of promoting allied sectors like poultry, dairy, fisheries and forestry for enhancing employment. Micro strategies may concentrate on a few selected growth engines, particularly infrastructure to help rural growth. At the same time labour market failures be avoided and employment be made available in all seasons by adjustment process. Even credit, market failures, commodity and product market failures be removed so as to create more jobs for the poor and unemployed.

Prof. Naidu also discussed in support led social security programmes followed by government of India in section IV: Eg. Land reforms, wage employment, self employment (IRDP); primary education, basic (JRY) health services, PDS, reservation for some classes. Protective social security measures implemented have been reviewed and the plus and minus points have been indicated for each scheme and in every state. These have been continued in 2002-2003 budget also which are expected to help the deprived and vulnerable sections of society.

The effectiveness of social security programmes was critically examined by the authors in section five. The main problems are: insufficient allocation of funds and its inefficient utilisation by the government both at centre and states and also by NGOs. They have righty observed that the State government should allot more funds particularly poorer states like Bihar, UP, MP, Rajasthan and Orissa (BIMARU States). Some states have done well in this direction; Eg. Kerala in health and education, Tamil Nadu in

Midday Meal Scheme.

The surprising observation by the authors is that since the reforms, allocation on social services and poverty alleviation programmes, have been declining contrary to the statements made by the government. Even as a share of GDP, Social sector expenditure has not shown increase in the reform period (first generation reforms) except in 1999-2000. The share in 1990 was lower than in 1980s; but as a proportion of total expenditure the share of social sector indicated rise since mid 1990s.

It appears that Centre has done better than States in post reform period, mainly due to withholding money from the States. In other words, the central schemes increased during 1990s and even in 2002 at the expense of allocation to the states. In rural development expenditure, the Centre moved away from rural employment to rural housing, water, rural roads etc. and on to basic minimum services. This shift favours human development or improvement of basic needs. The expenditure on health not changed much both at the centre and states and the percentage of spending on education even declined from 4.1% in 1990-91 to 3.8% in 1998-99, and the same trend is to be seen in the States.

International aid has shown increase on children but under-utilisation of funds is the problem due to absence of matching funds. Compared to other countries, social sector spending in India is low to other developing countries, to east Asian countries and low compared to UNDP prescribed ratios. The Reform process caused withdrawal of the state from economic activities, but this has to be reversed and higher amounts be allocated by government for social security of labour.

Two pertinent observations have been made: (1) There is urgent necessity to hike social sector spending by government, and (2) The effectiveness of many central and state sector schemes is poor.

These gaps must be attended by government, both at the centre and the states, and help the poor live a higher quality of life that is needed for an average person. The role of government, instead of being withdrawn, has to be increased and proper monitoring mechanism evolved to oversee the effective spending of allocations made for social security programmes for the labour so as to overcome deprivation and vulnerability and to lead a better quality of life. The right of a person to employment and decent living should be the fundamental right to be honoured by the government and take steps to implement its policies to achieve the goal of employment for all for sustainable development and living.

Velayutham Sarvanan critically analysed in his paper about the impact of social security initiatives relating to women beedi workers in rural areas in Tamil Nadu. They are exploited severely by the ownes of beedi factories, its agents or middlemen all over India. To prove effectively his idea and aim Dr. Saravanan selected one village (katteri) for the study based on the highest concentration of Beedi industries and workers. The village is located in the erstwhile North Arcot District of Tamil Nadu.

There are many studies on Beedi workers in Tamil Nadu particularly in the last decade, focussing on North Arcot District. The studies emphasized on the socio-economic conditions, child labour and health problem etc. both in rural and urban areas.

The earlier studies also focussed as pointed out by Dr. Sarvanana on socio-economic conditions of Beedi workers in the different parts of the country. They pinpoint to their regular struggle for survival while continuing in this occupation inspite of low wage irregular employment, and different forms of exploitation by the middlement and agents; lack of credit, education and medical facilities and neglect of government. Their conditions has not improved to a better level despite many legislations and the efforts of trade unions. This shows the sufferings of Weaker sections in society due to their own debility and failure of government in the effective implementation of their policies.

Beedi workers form part of unorganised workers whose share accounts for 93% in the total work force in India in

2002. These sections of workers are deprived of benefits like provident fund, dearness allowance, wage for holidays, maternity benefits, credit facilities at the all India level. Government has enacted several laws to protect the unorganised workers and implemented many social security schemes for their betterment; but not much improvement could be witnessed in the quality of life of these type of workers. The existing schemes cover old age pensions, maternity benefits and assistance to landless agricultural labourers and destitute women. But the legislation and the state oriented social security programmes have not produced the expected results in general and in particular relating to women in the unorganised sector. With the above scenario of the past, or Sarvananan made an attempt to analyse the impact of social security schemes for women beedi workers in rural areas of Tamil Nadu and in particular to women in Katteri village in the former north Arcot District with headquarters at Vellore.

The main objective of Saravana's article was the study of the impact of Social security initiatives for women beedi workers in his study area. Before actually attempting this work, the author explained in section II the growth and changing pattern of beedi industries in the North Arcot district, in section III covered Trade unionism and social security initiatives and in section IV analysed Tamil Nadu government policies like enactment of act and implementation of different schemes for women beedi workers.

In section V, Dr. Saravanan thoroughly analysed the impact of social security initiatives for women beedi workers both in terms of protective and promotional measures in the North Arcot District in terms of wages, other benefits, health conditions, awareness of beedi workers and problems of beedi workers.

Though since 1970s, the government has fixed the minimum wages for rolling 1000 beedies, yet the workers never got the statutory wage from the owners or agents who continue to exploit the beedi workers in their own.

way. The main drawback is that the beedi workers are not generally aware of the minimum wages act and their rights which lapse help the agents to exploit the workers to the maximum. Their economic power of beedi workers is very weak and hence prove for exploitation.

Since 1980s government implemented many schemes (other benefits) like pension, bonus, housing, medical facilities, scholarships for the children, maternity benefits etc. But only a very low percentage of beedi workers have availed these benefits; for example: Bonus (34%), P. Fund (2%), maternity benefit (1%), scholarship (1%) and in other schemes no worker was benefited.

Beedi workers suffer from many health problems like back pain, swelling of legs, cough, TB, gynic problems etc., Most of the beedi workers were treated either at private or government hospitals. Only 2% of workers surveyed visited the hospital and in general the beedi workers were not getting/taking treatment from government hospital due to distance and larger time for healing.

Only a small percentage of beedi workers are aware of the government facilities provided to them, the main cause being lack of social and political developments.

The beedi workers suffer from many problems as they work, on the leaves supplied by agents and contractors and work under their direct supervision. Hence they are treated like slaves by the owners. Workers usually migrate after marriage, the contractors also change the workers very often. The beedi workers are not entitled to avail the social security benefits and hence their productivity is undermined technically resulting in the denial of statutory benefits in the rural areas.

Based on the incisive study, Dr. Saravanan made a few suggestions like abolition of contractor or agent, all the beedi workers should be brought into account, they must be extended cooperative system at the village level to avoid exploitation. These type of statutory arrangements it is hoped would be mostly helpful to workers but would definitely enhance the value of government and its policies.

3. Dr. B. Vanitha concentrated on the social security provided to workers in the construction activity with a field survey conducted in Coimbatore, selecting 250 construction workers. Naturally it has more relevance in the sense that the findings are based on the data collected from the field workers.

Construction sector contributes heavily to economic development as it covers activities like irrigation, energy, road transport and telecommunications besides including social infrastructure like education, health and shelter building. As it covers a wide area and fields construction sector is considered as the second largest economic activity in India next only to agriculture. Moreover it generates higher incremental value per unit of investment then any other industry. This sector accounts for nearly 3.5% of the work force and is projected to expand at the rate of 5% per annum (NICMAR). The peculiar feature of the construction workers is that three fourths of the work force are unskilled and one seventh are skilled workers; only one in twenty are technicians. The work force is divided into three segments—Mandi, institutions and intermediaries.

In Coimbatore the prevalent system is mandi workers, that is, people who assemble at well-defined places from where the employer picks up the required worker. The author of the article indicated that the workers are suffering from health problems—skin disease, fever, cough, eye sore, asthma, breathing problem, body pain—and the workers go to private doctors to secure relief. The wages of construction workers are very low—Rs. 90 for Male and Rs. 60 for female per day. Hence their financial position is very weak. Most of the construction workers are illiterate and unskilled and they face many work hazards and are highly accident prone. The workers savings ability is very meagre as they get very low wages which are sufficient for their daily living only.

All in all, the author advocates government sponsored social security measures for construction workers as their financial empowerment is weak, educational level is low and skill worth is general in nature unless government takes up the cause of construction workers to provide necessary social security measures to protect them from sickness, unhealthy conditions, general diseases etc., their position is working society would deteriorate and degenerate which is not good in the interest of peaceful society.

4. Jayashree Dam P. Chaudhury covered in her paper the social security for workers in Guwahati (Assam state) urban market. She explained the distinction between formal and informal sectors and reasoned out the causes for the growth of unorganised sector. She also discussed briefly about rural unorganised and urban unorganised sector.

She empirically tested on Guwahati urban market by interviewing six persons excluding the owners. The interview revealed that workers in the unorganised sector highly suffer from wage/salary insecurity, exploited by employers and work in unhealthy places. Mrs. Chaudhury gave details of workers with salary experience, age, qualification etc., working in Guwahati and observed that the workers require social security for the smooth running of the State economy and to realise the objective of "Growth with Equality."

The author advocated the need to introduce social security schemes for workers of urban unorganised sector. She gave a few suggestions for government of Assam for implementation.

5. Dr. S.P. Singh dealt at length the Social security made available to rural labour through institutions. He devided his paper into five sections; introduction, concept of social security, existing provisions, institutional arrangement and conclusions.

In the introduction he explained briefly the reasons to protect the poor rural workers from personal and covariate risks so as to improve their living standards. In this context there is need to develop effective social security programmes and institutional arrangement to implement these programmes.

Dr. Singh defined social security, in the second section, drawing from ILO, Dreze and Sen. He analysed the existing provision in the III section like (a) promotional measures like IRDP (1980), TRYSEM (1979), DWCRA (1983), self employment programmes; JRY (1989) EAS (1993) wage employment programmes; (b) protective measures mostly covering the unorganised labour like landless Agricultural Labour Group Insurance Scheme, National Social Assistance programme, under which three schemes are implemented such as National Old Age Pension scheme, National Family Benefit Scheme and National Maternity Benefit Scheme. There are also other schemes like Rural Group Insurance Scheme, Food for Education programme, Annupurna Scheme, and Old Age Social and Income Security. In 2001 government of India in collobaration with LIC launched an ambitions Krishi Shramik Samajik Suraksha Yojana for agricultural labourers. He also indicated welfare schemes made for rural labour by Gujarat, Kerala, Andhra Pradesh, Tamil Nadu and Karnataka. He concludes after discussion that social security has both central and regional dimensions. According to him some states are doing well in the field of social security by making adequate provision through grass roots planning. He further states that the unorganised sector workers largely depend on the redistributive and poverty alleviation types of social security nets. The drawback, he points out, is lack of proper coordination and cohesion in the distribution of funds which needs an effective delivery mechanism for securing appropriate results.

In section IV, Dr. Singh discusses institutional arrangement. There are four categories (Jutting 1999) of social security systems adopted in developing countries, they are: State based systems, market based systems, member organisations based systems and private household based systems. The author examined the systems followed in India and quotes from H.D.R. of 1990 for taxing rural rich, so far not touched by government, to fund the social security programmes for rural poor; This is a controversial subject not amenable for easy solution. Many Central Sponsored schemes were critically examined by him including DRDA which has to be diswanted for securing better benefits to the poor. He advocates strengthening of PRIS so as to financially strengthen them for directly extending socially security benefits to the poor at the village level. He is also favourable for setting up institutions, like Grameena Bank run by Prof Yunus of Bangladesh in India. SEWA type voluntary organisation organised by unorganised workers since 1972 by Ela R. Bhat had improved the earning capacity of its members besides providing health care, child care insurance and shelter services to its members. Such institutions are rare to be found as many voluntary organisations have earned bad name by diverting the government grants sanctioned for the purposes not connected to the poor. Market based systems have not developed in India.

In section V, Dr. Singh offers concluding remarks and as an overview suggests an institutional frame work for efficient and cost effective delivery of various promotional and protective social security programmes. He wanted to make PRIs effective so as to provide efficient social security benefits to the unorganised workers mostly living in rural areas.

Rural labour in India has been gaining increasing attention from several points of view, more so for the rise in casual labour who have to be satisfied with seasonal employment for about one hundred twenty days in a year. Naturally they need social security of higher magnitude. Dr. Vipla Chopra in her paper tried to analyse the different aspects of social security relating to rural labour.

6. She explained that ILO has given top priority to social security as nearly 60 per cent of 200 million labour force in the world are unprotected, out of which 77% are living in developing countries. Briefly she touched how social security is introduced in Germany (originated in 1881), Austria, Hungary, Norway, European countries, USA, Newzealand and U.K. mostly due to the efforts of ILO. She also included the definition of social security in her paper.

In India social security was introduced only after 1947 and plan documents remained silent except in Ninth Plan.

Organised workers (7% of total employment) were covered by protective social security measures and the balance 93% in the unorganised sector were covered with promotional measures. Brief history of evolution of social security was also discussed from 1923 covering benefits like provident fund, gratuity and ESI benefits such as medical benefit, sickness benefit, disablement benefit, maternity benefit, dependents benefit and the funeral benefit—all to organised sector workers only. Recently GOI began to extend some of the benefits enjoyed by organised workers to the poorest of the poor in the organised sector. They are: pensions, survivor benefits (equivalent to family pension on the death of retired employees) and maternity benefits. Many State Governments also attempted to provide various protective social security measures for the unorganised poor and vulnerable sections of the society. In the 2001-2002 budget, the Insurance Regulatory and Development Authority (IRDA) was instituted to start a new pension scheme for the unorganised workers. In 2002-03 budget, a new corporations for Agricultural Insurance was proposed by the public sector general Insurance Companies. This may strengthen the presently very weak agricultural insurance.

Dr. V. Chopra also discussed about types of social securities in India like Income security, Employment security, Land security, Food and Nutritional security, Education security and other forms of security supported by official data. The recent programmes, meant for rural labour by way of security introduced by GOI, are: (a) Jawahar Gram Samridhi Yojana (JGSY), Sampoorna Grameena Rojgar Yojana (SGRY), Swarna Jayanthi Gram Swarozgar Yojana (SGSY), pradhana Manthri Gramodaya Yojana (PMGY), Krishi Shramik Samajik Suraksha Yojana, Shiksha Sahayog Yojana, National Agricultural Insurance scheme. All these programmes were briefly narrated. If the author had critically analysed the impact of their programmes on the rural labour in India that would have made a better effective and useful presentation.

Lastly, Dr. Vipla Chopra gave a few valuable suggestions

for enhancing social security of labour. The policy makers may go through these suggestions to rectify any loopholes in the existing schemes and take steps to make the benefits reach the rural unorganised poor labourers to live a better life. The Tenth Five year Plan after examining the recommendations of labour Commission report recently submitted to government in June 2002, would, it is hoped, introduce social security measures for increasing the protection in a substantiable way as a National Labour policy directive for the betterment of rural informal sector labour.

Prof. S. Vijayakumar and Dr. G. Subbayamma in their article on **"Social Security for Women Workers in India"** critically examined with analytical vigour various Central Government promotional programmes like JRY, IRDP, TRYSEM, DWCRA, EGS as well as protective social security measures for women (unorganized) workers. They also analysed the impact of structural adjustment on women workers.

It is true that social security for women workers is not provided either by government or employers and other institutions as the problem demands and to the required level though, the women workers share in the employment at the national level works out to 50% and their importance and significance are very much emphasized and recognized. Only oral support is extended to this important section of employees and the government has to translate oral statements into effective actions. Keeping this in view, the authors made an attempt to evaluate the social security measures extended to women workers. As there are many deficiencies in the provision of social security content to women workers, they argued for effective implementation of anti-poverty programmes by the Central Government, overcoming the confusion and complexity associated with them. The authors desired introduction of a comprehensive social security programmes at the National level and decentralized operation of such a programme with the help of NGO's so as to benefit the poor women workers. The women workers need effective, protective social security measures from employers—either public, private, corporate etc., in particular to those working in unorganised sectors to make them effective and efficient contributors to the development of country's economy as in the case of developed countries. Gender discrimination in the provision of social security measures has to be totally discouraged by heavy puritive measures for violation of the rules prescribed by Government in this direction.

1

ECONOMIC REFORMS AND SOCIAL SECURITY OF LABOUR IN INDIA

K. M. Naidu, K. Srinivasulu Naidu and
Mrs. P. Manjushree Naidu

In the context of implementation of economic reforms, the experts on Labour studies began to know the impact of reforms on social security of workers, more so on the labour working in the unorganised sector. So much so the study in this direction has received higher attention from academics, policy makers, multilateral organisations and non-governmental organisations. It has gained the status of a growth industry (see Van Ginnerkan 1997, 1998, Jhabwala and Subramanya 2000, Seeta Prabhu 2001).

As the economy undergoes change and as societies develop, there emerges a need for social security to those who lack an income due to disability, old age, death of main earner, maternity, unemployment, injury at work place etc. The Government in India as in other developing countries have small programmes and not very extensive and hence cover only a small part of working population not exceeding 10% the organised sector. Even here the amounts allotted are meagre and being reduced every year since 1990 when even the government experienced resource crunch. The interest in this subject of social security gained much significance after the award of Nobel Prize in Economics to Prof. Amartya K. Sen in 1998 for his outstanding contributions in the field of welfare economics and his stress on capability, empowerment, entitlement, efficient allocation of resources, poverty removal, equal opportunities for all, freedom from hunger, poverty, unemployment etc. Social Security is used in a broader sense in developing countries than that is observed in developed countries. The content of social security measures differ depending on country's economic development. On the whole the social security made available by government or private effort helps in raising the living standards of the people that are covered. The paper attempts to analyse the spread and impact of social security in India after implementation of economic reforms. The definition and issues on social security of labour is covered in section-2, how the growth promoting policies help the labour is explained in section 3, the support-led social security programmes are analysed in section 4 and last section (5) examines the effectiveness of social security programmes.

Definition and Issues

The Beveridge Committee Report (1942) defines social security as "Freedom from want". But in practice its provision was confined to only three aspects—Children's allowances, comprehensive health and rehabilitation services and maintenance, of employment to avoid mass unemployment.[1] The most authoritative definition on social security emerged from the efforts of ILO (Parott 1992) and led to identification of costs of social security provisions (with the heads on which the social security departments of public bodies incurred expenditures and the costs in different countries were published in 1952 at the 35th session of International Labour Conference of the social security (minimum standards) convention (102). According to ILO the term social security has been used to refer to "the result achieved by a comprehensive and successful series of measures for protecting the public (or a large sector of it) from the economic distress that, in the absence of such measures, would be caused by the stoppage of earnings in sickness, unemployment or old age and after death, for making available to the same public, medical care as needed and for subsidising families bringing up young children."[2] The above definition's aim is provision of relief mainly to workers from particular contingencies and actions. The circumstances which forced the adoption of definition were forgotten and the institutional definition was accepted as the official definition of the ILO. In this process the emphasis by the Beveridge Committee Report on freedom from want was sidelined. The net result is that the social security measures are mostly confined to the organised sector workers only. Even here the record of government of India by way of budgetary allocation as well as legislative measures and its implementation leave much to be desired as they are inadequate and less than needed. Moreover in India 90% of Indian workers are to be found working in unorganised sector whose coverage was completely neglected. The economic reforms initiated by government were mainly meant to benefit the elite and richer section of society and hence mostly neglected poor and weaker sections in the society and labour markets in India. The suffering of these people instead of reducing steadily increased after the implementation of economic reforms.

Increasing interest in economic globalisation led to increasing interest envinced by developing countries and development organisations like UNDP and the world Bank resulting in newer concepts and approaches in social security. The Western idea about social security does not cover high degree of deprivation and valunderability of the majority of population seen in developing countries. Discussion on social security began to emphasize on social risk management and human security. This necessitated public measures to help individuals, households, communities and groups in managing income risks to reduce vulnerability, improve consumption, and enhance equity while making efforts to develop the economy, while income security and human security to overcome deprivation so as to ensure the safety of all people (through better standard of living) and this led to thinking on social structures and practices. Social security has to be seen, therefore, in terms of safety from chronic threats like hunger, disease and protection from sudden and heartful descriptions in the regular daily life—maybe in homes, in jobs or in communities (UNDP, 1994). It took security to mean methods to promote human development and defined it in terms of protection against human deprivation. Human development is taken as a social security measure. But the latter mainly aim at removing vulnerability by preventing a decline in living standards in general and promoting basic living standards during economic failures.

As per the scientific view the concern with social security is mainly related to direct role that public action can play in reducing human deprivation and eliminating vulunerability in developing countries. The emphasis is on the use of efficient means (publication) to follow necessary objectives (reduction of deprivation and vulnerability). This action is justified because "many developing countries have large shares of employment in unorganised/informal sectors and workers in this sector do not have access to the benefits of traditional social security measures."[3]

The Issues

The organised sector covers Government sector, the public sector and the private organised sector. The workers in this three categories have the facility of conventional types of social security schemes. In the nineties nearly 26 million workers were organised out of 262.3 million workers (10%) in India. Social security schemes in the organised sector are divided into three types (a) employees' liability scheme, (b) Social relevance schemes and (c) Provident funds. Even these schemes are not working well as found in the government report; eg. The Maharashtra's Employment State Insurance Scheme reported that the ESIs is not helping the beneficiaries. The schemes suffers from corruption and the facilities in the hospitals are very poor besides the negligence of those concerned. Moreover the workers are dissatisfied with ESIS scheme due to its inadequate funds, lack of coverage, callousness of officials and doctors, insufficient medicines, improper care etc. Inspite of these difficulties, there is some help from government for organised workers, but one can see total negligence of workers in the unorganised sector.

There are six types of unorganised rural labour (Sankaran 1996) like agricultural labours, weavers, rural artisms, fishermen, salt workers, construction workers etc., besides workers in urban informal sector, in which majority form migrants from rural labour in search of employment in urban areas. Nearly 93% of workers were in unorganised sector in 1999-2000 (See table No. 1). Even in manufacturing sector, more than 80% of total workers were in the unorganised sector. Likewise service sector has large share of unorganised workers.

TABLE 1
ORGANISED AND UNORGANISED WORKERS AND PERCENTAGE SHARE OF UNORGANISED WORKERS IN THE TOTAL: 1999-2000

Sector	*Organised workers (millions)*	*Unorganised workers (millions)*	*Total workers (millions)*	*Share of Unorganised sector (per cent)*
Ag. allied activities	1.39	236.11	237.61	99.42
Mining quarrying	1.01	1.25	2.26	55.31
Manufacturing incl. Repair services	6.79	37.27	44.02	84.67
Electricity, gas and water	1.00	0.05	1.05	4.76
Construction	1.18	16.41	17.59	93.29
Trade, hotel & restaurants	0.49	40.77	41.26	98.81
Transport, Storage & Communication	3.15	11.59	14.74	78.63
Financial Services	1.65	3.37	5.02	67.13
Community, social & personal services	11.49	21.95	33.44	65.64
All Sectors (Total)	28.11	368.89	397.00	92.92

Source: Computed from GOI (2001).

Inspite of shift to non-form sector in rural areas, agriculture has 71% of males and 85% of females. After inclusion of urban areas, agriculture accounts for 60% of workers in 1999-2000 (see Table No. 2). This points to dominance of unorganised sector in agriculture.

TABLE 2
SECTORAL DISTRIBUTION OF WORKERS AT ONE DIGIT LEVEL: RURAL INDIA, 1977-78 to 1999-2000

Sectors	*1977-78*	*1983*	*1987-88*	*1993-94*	*1999-2000*
Rural Persons					
Agriculture & Allied	83.4	81.5	78.3	78.4	76.3
Mining & Quarrying	0.4	0.5	0.6	0.6	0.5
Manufacturing	6.2	6.8	7.2	7.0	7.4
Electricity, gas & water	0.1	0.1	0.2	0.2	0.2
Construction	1.3	1.6	3.3	2.4	3.3
Trade, hotels and restaurants	3.3	3.4	4.0	4.3	5.1
Transport, storage, community	0.8	1.1	1.3	1.4	2.1
Services	4.5	4.9	5.1	5.7	5.2
All	100.0	100.0	100.0	100.0	100.0
Rural Males					
Agriculture & Allied	80.7	77.8	74.6	74.0	71.4
Mining & Quarrying	0.5	0.6	0.7	0.7	0.6
Manufacturing	6.4	7.0	7.4	7.0	7.3
Electricity, gas & water	0.2	0.2	0.3	0.3	0.2
Construction	1.7	2.2	3.7	3.2	4.5
Trade, hotels and restaurants	4.0	4.4	5.1	5.5	6.8
Transport, storage, community	1.2	1.7	2.0	2.2	3.2
Services	5.3	6.1	6.2	7.1	6.1
All	100.0	100.0	100.0	100.0	100.0
Rural Females					
Agriculture & Allied	88.2	87.5	84.7	86.2	85.4
Mining & Quarrying	0.2	0.3	0.4	0.4	0.7
Manufacturing	5.9	6.4	6.9	7.1	7.6
Electricity, gas & water	–	–	–	–	–
Construction	0.6	0.7	2.7	0.8	1.1
Trade, hotels and restaurants	2.0	1.9	2.1	2.1	2.0
Transport, storage, community	0.1	0.1	0.1	0.1	0.1
Services	3.0	2.8	3.0	3.4	3.7
All	100.0	100.0	100.0	100.0	100.0

Source: Visaria, 1999 and NSSO 2000.

In the case of organised workers there is need for measures to protect their income in the circumstances that deprive them of income or to reduce it. But in the case of unorganised labour with no regular employment and assured income, the need is for employment security and improvement in quality of employment. In both the cases the primary concern is protection of regular income so as to make them live a better and quality life.

However, the major issues are:

(a) Low employment growth inspite of high GDP growth as growth of employment dropped from 2% per annum during 1983 to 1993-94 to less than one percent per annum between 1993-94 to 1999-2000. It means that post reforms period witnessed jobless growth, putting unemployed (including workers in closed units) to severe deprivation and low levels of living.

(b) The other important issue faced by workers is casualisation and marginalisation of workers, for eg. the percentage of casual labourers for males and females in rural areas rose by 11.8% (22 to 33.8%) and 7.3% (31.4 to 38.7%) respectively between 1972-73 and 1993-94. Similarly due to closure of many units substantial per cent of workers 20 to 50% have became marginalised pushing them to low levels of living and into social problems.

(c) The effect of jobless growth has been neutralised by self-employment process which is not without heavy burden on the poor and weaker sections of society. No doubt the proportion of self-employed declined, yet their percentage is very high at 53% in India in 1999-2000 and the same was 58%, 40% and 48% respectively in agriculture, secondary sector and tertiary sector.

(d) The sufferings of poor workers and the nature and quality of employment. Unemployment as such is not a problem in India. Workers in organised sector are thrown out of employment suddenly and face problem in finding alternative job simultaneously or after some time. This forces them to seek work in unorganised sector. Naturally many people are forced to work in unorganised sector whose nature and quality are: low earnings, poor working conditions, lack of (social security) protection, contract nature of work etc. Due to these characteristics the incidence of poverty is highest for casual labour in both rural and urban areas. In 1993-94 (and even 1999-2000 as per World Bank Study) 50% of casual workers were below poverty line (49.2% in rural areas and 57% in urban areas). As per NSS data latest round (43) the incidence of poverty declined during the last decade (Table 3). But the World Bank Study estimated for 1999-2000 that 50% of people are living below poverty line which applies equally to workers. The only saving point is that rate of decline in poverty share was the lowest for casual workers and highest for regular workers.[4] It is therefore to be inferred that casualisation be related to marginalisation and immiseration in the form of low income and poor living. The other observation is that suffering from poverty for casual labourers and self employed was more than that experienced by the unemployed.

TABLE 3
INCIDENCE OF POVERTY FOR WORKERS AND UNEMPLOYED: 1983 to 1993-94(%)

Worker Types	*Rural*			*Urban*		
	1983	*1987-88*	*1993-94*	*1983*	*1987-88*	*1993-94*
Self Employed	38.5	32.4	28.3	44.3	41.2	34.0
Regular Employed	32.7	26.5	17.5	26.9	24.5	18.3
Casual Labourers	59.3	52.0	49.4	62.9	63.9	57.0
Total Workers	44.8	38.4	35.2	40.8	38.4	32.0
Unemployed	33.0	38.5	21.1	40.1	36.0	27.1

Source: Estimated by the author based on NSS data.

Growth Promoting Policies

Beside on the economic strength of the economy, a country adopts a programme. To suit their convenience different schemes are advocated. Two approaches have been suggested by Dreze and Sen (1989) for raising the living standards of workers. The first approach emphasises on promotion of economic growth to raise private and public incomes. This they called as 'Growth mediated security'. The second is named by them as 'support led-security'. In the latter higher support is extended to areas like employment provision, income redistribution, health care, education and social assistance to help improve distribution without waiting for a change in the level of general efficiencey.[5] Government effort alone is insufficient to provide social and economic security to the poor. Hence there is need for public and private cooperation to effectively implement growth mediated and support led security measures. Private effort means steps taken by private business firms, NGOs, community based organisations etc.

Broadly the government followed a dual policy strategy in providing social security for the organised workers (10% of work force) 7% as on March 2002 as out of 40 crore workers, the organised sector forms only 2.8 crores. In this 86 lakh workers are in private sector (3%) and the balance 97% are in private sector (Bharat Junjunwala, The Ecenadu, March 23; 2002 p. 3). The government implemented many social security schemes through different legislations. These schemes are mostly funded by employers and some by employees. Employers' liability is for accident relief and maternity benefits, social insurance for health benefits through contributions from employers and employees; social assistance through welfare fund legislations funded through taxes on employers, retired benefits like provident fund, pension and gratuity, which are saving schemes are made available with joint contributions from employees and employers. Excepting gratuity, all these schemes are mostly funded by employers and administered by government. Eg. 12% of wages on provident fund, 4.81% by way of gratuity,

4% by way of ESI contribution, and 8.33% (loss making units) up to 20% (profit making units) by way of loans are contributed by employers. The total cost to companies on social security and welfare benefits account for 40% of the wage bill.[6] Apart from these benefits, employees run mutual benefit thrift societies, consumer cooperatives with support from employers.

India depended on both growth promoting and support led policies to help the unorganised workers. In the case of support led policies the country relied on promotional measures like self-employment and wage employment programmes, general health, education etc. It is practically impossible, financially unfeasible to cover with social security benefits for all the poor workers as the poor are so large and their problems so massive. Even the programme of unemployment benefit in India would be highly costly and administratively complex. Hence India relied on promotional forms, direct anti-poverty programmes, as against protective interventions.

Growth promoting policies emphasize and aim at increasing employment opportunities and quality of employment which are expected to improve social and economic security for the unorganised workers. This means policy thrust for growth as well as structural changes in the economy as a whole (GOI 2001). The task force on Employment opportunities (GOI 2001) identified five areas which form the strategy for employment generation. They are (1) accelerating the rate of growth of GDP particularly the sectors whose spread will help low income segments of labour force (2) appropriate sectoral policies in individual sectors, (3) implementation of particular special programmes for creating additional employment, helping vulnerable groups (by passed by general growth policies, 4) adopting appropriate policies for education and skill development to upgrade quality of labour force so as to create high quality jobs, (5) ensuring that the policy and legal conditions relating to labour market encourage labour absorption, particularly in the organised sector (GOI 2001). In these 1, 2, and 4 relate to growth promoting and skill improvement policies and 3 relates to support led policies, but 5 pertains only to organised sector. In the growth promoting security policy, the government role is limited to as facilitator or motivator for private investment and for skill improvements.

The growth promoting policies need support from removal of anti-poor laws, setting right market failures and adoption of appropriate macro and micro strategies.

Anti-poor laws have to be rectified to help the poor person, farmer, small trade to establish units of their own. eg. tribals should cultivate land with the support of forest laws, a farmer and a trader should be able to establish without a licence a brick plant, a rice shelling plant, cold storage etc to increase non-farm activities in the rural areas.

Macro strategies should concentrate on growth of agriculture particularly in rainfed areas so that labour force may move from agriculture to rural non-farm activities which would also reduce rural poverty. The sub or allied sectors like poultry, dairy, fisheries and forestry be promoted to increase employment.

Relating to micro strategies, there is need to concentrate on a few selected growth engines. Infrastructure facilities in rural areas be sufficiently improved to help rural growth.

Labour market failures be avoided by shortage of agricultural labour in coastal region and in urban manual activities coexist with a large amount of seasonal unemployment in dry areas; unemployment for powerlooms and handloom workers coexist with a shortage of garment workers at approach export parks. Such failures be eliminated.

Even credit market failure, commodity and product market failure be removed. Infrastructure constraints like lack of power, communication facilities hamper growth activities. Here, government and private effort in unision remove the failures to create more jobs for the benefit of the poor and unemployed.

Support Led Social Security Programmes

India adopted the following schemes as support-led security programmes.

1. Land reforms and its equitable distribution to help the poor residing in rural areas.
2. Promotional social security programmes like:
   (a) Wage employment programmes like EGS, JRY.
   (b) Self employment programmes like IRDP and SGSY.
   (c) Providing basic needs: primary education, basic health services etc.
   (d) Public distribution system, PDS, and nutrition programmes such as Integrated Development Services (ICDS) and midday meal schemes.
   (e) Elimination of social exclusion: Reservation for some classes.

   Some of the above programmes may also be taken as protective measures.
3. Protective social security measures: These are provided both at the National and State level with the aim of giving financial cushion against unexpected poverty suffered by the poor that seriously affects them like sickness, accidents, old age and maturity, flood damage etc. Table-4 gives various social security and welfare schemes implemented at the State level. Prasad in 1995 (p 794) presented a review of these social security schemes (relating to unorganised labour) in different states in India. Broadly, observations are:
   (a) All states implemented old age pension schemes. Some states like Andhra Pradesh, Gujarat, Kerala, and Tamil Nadu have special pension schemes for agricultural labour.
   (b) Tamil Nadu, Kerala, Gujarat and Orissa have pension schemes for poor widows and the physically handicapped.
   (c) Maharashtra is unique in the introduction of an employment guarantee scheme, but States like

TABLE 4
LIST OF VARIOUS SOCIAL SECURITY AND WELFARE SCHEMES AT THE STATE LEVEL

1. *Old age pension*
   Andhra Pradesh (1960)
   Assam (1983)
   Bihar (1970)
   Gujarat (1978)
   Haryana
   Himachal Pradesh (1968)
   Jammu and Kashmir (1976)
   Karnataka (1965)
   Kerala (1960)
   Madhya Pradesh (1970)
   Maharashtra (1980)
   Orissa (1975)
   Punjab (1968)
   Rajasthan (1964)
   Tamil Nadu (1962)
   Uttar Pradesh (1957)
   West Bengal (1964)
2. *Pension for agricultural landless labourers*
   Andhra Pradesh (1984)
   Gujarat (1981)
   Kerala (1982)
   Tamil Nadu (1981)
3. *Destitute women*
   Tamil Nadu (1975, 1986)
4. *Maternity benefit*
   Gujarat (1975, 1986)
   Karnataka (1984)
   Kerala
5. *Physically disabled*
   Haryana
   Gujarat (1978)
   Kerala (1982)
   Tamil Nadu (1974)
   West Bengal
6. *Health and Medical under voluntary agencies*
   Maharashtra
   Tamil Nadu
   Voluntary health services (1963)
7. *Employment*
   Maharashtra (EGS)

8. *Relief for the educated unemployed*
   Gujarat (1979)
   Kerala (1982)
   Maharashtra (1979)
   Tamil Nadu (1980)
   West Bengal (1985)
9. *Self employment*
   Kerala (1982)
   Maharashtra (1980)
   Tamil Nadu (1985-86)
   Gujarat (1981)
10. *Group insurance schemes*
   Gujarat
   Kerala
   Maharashtra
   Orissa
   Tamil Nadu
   Bihar
   West Bengal
   Karnataka

Source: Statistical Abstracts and Economic Surveys at State Level, Various Issues.

Tamil Nadu, Kerala and Gujarat have unemployment relief schemes.

(d) Maternity benefits for landless agricultural labour have been implemented in Gujarat, Karnataka and Kerala to balance loss of wage due to absence at work allowance, though paid for first and second issues only.

(e) Health care is not extended to workers in any state. Gujarat, Tamil Nadu and Maharashtra have some welfare schemes only for women and children, while many states provide welfare benefits for different types of population below poverty line.7

Table 5 presents a picture of coverage schemes for selected states. It is to be inferred that the beneficiaries covered are very meagre and expenditure incurred is quite small compared to the magnitude. Despite this drawback, the attempt made by some states to provide social security

TABLE 5
BENEFICIARIES AND EXPENDITURE FOR VARIOUS SOCIAL SECURITY SCHEMES

	Old Age Pension (OAP)		*Assistance to Widows*		*Assistance to Disabled*		*Pension to Agri-cultural Workers*		*Unemployment Relief*	
Year/State and Scheme	*Bene-ficiaries*	*Expendi-ture*	*Bene-ficiaries*	*Expendi-ture*	*Bene-ficiaries*	*Expendi-ture*	*Bene-ficiaries*	*Expendi-ture*	*Bene-ficiaries*	*Expendi-ture*
1	2	3	4	5	6	7	8	9	10	11
Gujarat										
1989-90	56,470	5.63	1,813	20.96	865	6.35				
1990-91	58,622	9.05	2,437	33.33	1,445	1.09				
1991-92	63,658	9.04	2,883	66.24	1,088	1.31				
Kerala										
1988-89	57,321	13.47	1,20244		66,764	69.84	30,06,347		2,15,456	23.54
1989-90	58,115	11.79	1,24,355		73,835	69.86	3,02,312		2,46,040	19.96
1990-91	27,795	12.77	1,33,401		77,372	87.52	3,23,781		2,64,314	19.35
Maharashtra										
1989-90	3,21,576	41.57	–						14,183	4.96
1990-91	3,40,557	41.46	–						12,206	5.29
1991-92	3,28,592	50.17	–						12,140	5.51
Orissa										
1989-90	1,00,000	7.57	40,000	3.03	20,000	113				
1990-91	89,847	9.07	62,994	6.36	20,000	202				
1991-92	1,30,422	16.45	1,93,026	24.34	30,000	292	76,707	9.67		

Cont.

Year/State and Scheme	Old Age Pension (OAP)		Assistance to Widows		Assistance to Disabled		Pension to Agricultural Workers		Unemployment Relief	
	Beneficiaries	*Expenditure*	*Beneficiaries*	*Expenditure*	*Beneficiaries*	*Expenditure*	*Beneficiaries*	*Expenditure*	*Beneficiaries*	*Expenditure*
1	2	3	4	5	6	7	8	9	10	11
Tamil Nadu										
1989-90	1,71,9722	103.1	1,28,820	90.9 (e)						
1990-91	2,13,213	122.3	1,60,997	105.3 (e)						
1991-92	2,32,821	133.7	1,91,140	205.9 (e)						

Notes: (a) Expenditures shown are in rupees lakh. (b) Data not available for all the districts. (c) Data includes widows also as Maharashtra has no special schemes for this. (d) Scheme for Agricultural labour introduced during 1991-92. (e) Includes pension to physically handicapped destitutes and destitute labour.

Source: Prasad (1995).

to unorganised labour is laudable and worthy of emulation by other states. Among the states listed in the table, Kerala extends all types of benefits (five) during 1989-90 to 1990-91, Orissa offered three schemes, old age pension, assistance to workers, assistance to the disabled between 1989-90 and 1991-92 and pension to agricultural workers only for 1991-92 and for 1991-92; Tamil Nadu provided help only for two schemes old age pension and assistance to workers during 1989-90 and 1991-92, Gujarat implemented three schemes between 1989-90 and 1991-92—Old age pension schemes, assistance to workers and assistance to the disabled; and Maharashtra adopted during the same period only two schemes old age pension and unemployment relief, the latter earned name at the all India level and recommended for implementation by other states.

The Union budget 1995-96 for the first time initiated 4 schemes to help the unorganised and vulnerable sections—(1) NABARD was authorised to open credit cooperative and RRB's were asked to met the credit needs of STs. (2) Loans to Khadi and village industries through banks; (3) NABARD extends refinancing to commercial banks for providing credit to cooperative handloom institutions; and (4) programme only for rural areas (a) building one million houses in 1995-96; (b) introduced natural social assistance scheme under which (a) minimum old age pension of Rs. 75 PM will be paid to people above 65 years of age, and below poverty line; (b) one time settlement amount of Rs. 5 thousand in the case of sudden death of primary bread-winner in the poor households, (c) pre and post-natal monetary care to poor women; (d) group LIG. Some of these schemes have been continued in the subsequent and the latest budget for 2002-03.[8] In this way, protective measures introduced in 1995-96 were continued at the National level. It would help the deprived and vulnerable sections of society if the allocation of funds are increased depending upon the success of implementation.

Effectiveness of Social Security Programmes

As discussed in the earlier pages, India adopted many promotional and protective social security schemes. The main problems are insufficient allocation of funds and its inefficient utilisation of funds by the governments (both state and central and also by NGOs). There is need for more funds for social security programmes in a poor country like India, compared to rich western countries and rich developing countries in Asia (Singapore, Malaysia). The State Governments should allot more funds particularly poorer states like MP, Bihar, UP, Rajasthan and Orissa (BIMARU States).

Besides higher allocation of funds, emphasis should be placed on effectiveness of the schemes touching upon efficient utilisation of funds and the reach of the same to poorer sections. The record of Kerala and Tamil Nadu bear this out amply. Keralas success story, inspite of being poor state in economic growth relates to efficient public action on health and education (basic needs) which enhanced standard of living of poor people. The efficiency lies in effective utilisation rather than in allocation of resources. Kerala's success owe partly to historical reasons. But the Malabar region, a part of Kerala, was much behind Travencore and Cochin when the state was formed in 1956; but this region levelled with other regions by 1980's (in social development) mainly due to state action and peoples own interest, besides public participation and local leadership (Ramachandran 1997). According to Kannan (1992), the Vigilance of different political parties and their unions and the adoption of strict measures in the village offices, have contributed to the success of social security measures and in particular payment of pensions to the poor. Perhaps some protective social security schemes might have helped remove the contingent poverty of some deprived sections of the people in the unorganised sector.

Tamil Nadu is a pioneer state in the implementation of nutrition scheme (mid day meal programme) and protective social security measures. The two successful security schemes are (a) C.M's Nutrition Meal Programme (CMNMP) and TN Integration Nutrition Project (TNIP); the first one, largest in the World, helped in the increase of nutrition of many school going children; the second one, a health-linked nutrition intervention scheme; was implemented in rural areas in a cost effective manner. There may be some faults in implementation in some areas of the Tamil Nadu, but the State did well in these social security schemes. Other States can learn from the success experience of Kerala and Tamil Nadu in the area of protective social security measures at affordable cost to help the vulnerable poor, avoiding the drawbacks found.

A few states also have taken initiatives in this direction. Eg. Employment Guarantee Schemes in Maharashtra, primary education scheme in Himachal Pradesh and Madhya Pradesh public distribution schemes in Andhra Pradesh and land reforms in West Bengal. However the less developed states like Bihar, UP and Rajasthan have not shown, for reasons unknown, interest to adopt social security programmes.

There is every need for the promotional and protective programmes of the government to reach the needy poor. This is possible through decentralisation access to information and social mobilisation on the top of active peoples participation.

Financing of Social Sector

Since the introduction of economic reforms, allocation on social services and poverty alleviation programmes have been declining (social sector expenditure) i.e., spending on Social Services and Rural development. Table 6, 7 and 8 reveal this tendency very clearly.[9]

As a share of GDP, social sector expenditure has not shown increase during the reform period (first generation reforms) except in 1999-2000 for the states and centre taken together (Table 6), the share in 1990 were lower than in 1980s. But as a proportion of total expenditure, the share of social sector clearly indicated rise since mid 1990s.

TABLE 6
SOCIAL SECTOR (SOCIAL SERVICES + RURAL DEVELOPMENT) EXPENDITURE BY CENTRE AND STATES

	Social Sector Exp. (Revenue + Capital)			*Social Sector Exp. (Revenue)*	
Year	*As % of GDP*	*As % of Agg. Pub. Exp. (Rev.+ Capital)*	*Per capita exp (in Rs.) In 1993-94 prices*	*As % of GDP*	*As % of Agg. Pub. Exp.*
1	*2*	*3*	*4*	*5*	*6*
1987-88	7.74	25.29	562	7.23	31.23
1988-89	7.40	25.22	583	6.95	30.97
1989-90	7.64	25.19	633	7.23	30.98
1990-91	6.78	24.85	623	6.43	30.00
1991-92	6.58	24.28	599	6.21	28.54
1992-93	6.39	24.06	594	6.06	28.83
1993-94	6.46	24.58	623	6.16	29.09
1994-95	6.41	25.01	633	6.06	28.74
1995-96	6.40	25.95	675	6.10	29.51
1996-97	6.48	27.22	739	6.15	29.13
1997-98	6.60	26.95	789	6.29	30.01
1998-99	6.94	27.36	890	6.60	30.41
1999-2000(R)	7.55	27.69	1027	7.11	30.27
2000-01 (B)	6.97	26.61	959	6.54	29.29

R: revised; B: budget
Source: Estimated based on data from *Indian Public Finance Statistics,* GOI, 1995 and 2000-01.

Since 1993-94 the share of GDP pertaining to social sector was higher compared to 1990-91 (first year of reform though not much different viewed from 1980s (Table 7). It is a fact that as a proportion of public expenditure and as real per capital expenditure we observe a substantial rise in social sector spending since mid 1990s and higher compared to 1980s.

States expenditure as a proportion GSDP and aggregate expenditure, on social sector spending has declined (Table 8); no doubt in per capita real expenditure, there has been some rise, but not in the first half of 1990s and also not much for rural development.

TABLE 7
SOCIAL SECTOR (SOCIAL SERVICES + RURAL DEVELOPMENT) EXPENDITURE BY CENTRAL GOVERNMENT

Year	*As % of GDP*	*As % of Agg. Exp.*	*Per capita exp (in Rs.) In 1993-94 prices*
1986-87	1.61	7.47	113
1988-89	1.59	7.90	124
1990-91	1.42	7.55	130
1991-92	1.25	7.23	114
1992-93	1.29	7.70	119
1993-94	1.49	8.92	144
1994-95	1.49	9.26	147
1995-96	1.54	9.97	162
1996-97	1.56	10.48	177
1997-98	1.60	10.35	191
1998-99	1.67	10.39	213
1999-2000 (R)	1.59	10.22	216
2000-01 (B)	1.58	10.24	217

R: revised; B: budget
Source: Expenditure budgets of GOI, Vol. I.

TABLE 8
SOCIAL SECTOR EXPENDITURE (SOCIAL SERVICES + RURAL DEVELOPMENT) OF 25 STATES EXCL. NCT DELHI

Year	*As % of GSDP*	*As % of Aggregate Exp.*
1990-91	5.98	39.20
1991-92	5.85	37.20
1992-93	5.72	37.60
1993-94	5.57	35.64
1994-95	5.27	34.82
1995-96	5.33	37.31
1996-97	5.13	36.21
1997-98	5.18	36.52
1998-99	5.41	38.07
1999-2000	6.06	38.60
2000-01	5.46	35.80

Source: RBI Bulletins

It appears that Centre has done better than the states in post reform period; one caveat has to be added. Centre has withheld money from the States. The central schemes increased during 1990s and even in 2002 at the expenses of allocation (from overall plan outlay) to the states. In the social sector, however, the responsibility of the states are increasing compared to the central government.

There is a visible change in the composition of social sector spending both in the States and the Centre from 1996-97, a shift away from rural development. Even within rural development outlay at the centre, the government moved from rural employment schemes to rural housing, water, rural roads etc and on to basic minimum services. This indicates a shift from traditional ways (removal of poverty) to human development or improvement of basic needs.

Another fact to be known is that expenditure on health not changed much both at the centre and states. From 1990 to 1995 there is no change and after 1995 the per capital real expenditure on health by the States increased. The percentage spending on education declined from 4.1% in 1990-91 to 3.8% in 1998-99 (at the centre) and the trend is to be seen in the States.

In most states expenditure on social sector spending has not increased upto 1995, but in the second half increase is observed in terms of per capita real expenditure. The rich State (Goa) and middle income (West Bengal) states have shown better performance than the poor states. Within the poorer states, spending on social sector is better in MP, Orissa and Rajasthan, and very poor in Bihar and UP.

International aid has shown increase on children. There has been underutilisation to the extent of 10% of plan expenditure during end of the 1990s decade due to absence of matching funds, lack of local infrastructure or skills, lack of interest, delays in release of funds.

Compared to other countries, social sector spending in India is low; to other developing countries, to east Asian countries and also even low compared to UNDP prescribed ratios.

Whether the reform process caused withdrawal of the state from some economic activities. The answer is yes. But it is to be admitted that after 1995, more amounts have been allocated to social sector, yet as a share of GDP, spending has not shown increase; even if there is an improvement, it is only marginal.

The above analysis leads to two desirable statements. One, there is an immediate necessity to hike social sector spending by government, particularly in the context of 93rd Amendment to the Constitution by Lok Sabha regarding the right to education for children between 6-14 years of age, which need only a rise of one per cent of GDP per annum in the next ten years to. State and central government should evince interest (overcoming cuts in education spending as the first step) in allocating more amounts in budgets in tenth Five Year Plan Period. Public vigilance and demand is the only remedy that could achieve this aim.

Two, the effectiveness of many central and State sector schemes is poor. The mid-term appraisal of Ninth Plan has critically commented on this negligence and lapse of governments (GOI, 2000). The Planning Commission also never hides this fact of deterioration about the quality of governance of these schemes. The remedy lies in decentralisation, devolution, daring attitude of people at the grass-roots level, supported by young and dynamic leadership both in the administration and in the political parties.

Final Overview

Economic reforms are expected to benefit the labour both in the organised and unorganised sector. In actual practice the implementation of reforms (first generation) since 1990 has benefited mostly the elite and rich class, reforms mostly bypassed the deprived and vulnerable sections of society. The structural adjustment process and stabilisation of the economy aimed at by reforms were successfully completed. But the process resulted in jobless growth, removed of employed due to closure of uneconomic units, stoppage of new recruitment, forced removal of employed persons through VRS scheme etc. for the labor the gift of reforms is casualisation and marginalisation of labour, transformation of organised labour to unorganised labour, deprivation and vulnerability.

The government was expected to compensate the sufferings experienced by labour through social security measures. For organised labour constituting 10% of total labour, the social security measures were provided mostly by employers with small support from government and mainly through contributory schemes (employers and employees). The employers provide health benefits, housing, accident relief, pension etc. The government provide health facilities through ESIS schemes. However the amounts allotted are inadequate and the functioning of ESIS scheme is far from satisfactory.

In the case of unorganised sector two approaches are followed: (1) Growth promoting schemes; (2) Support oriented security schemes. The former creates employment for deprived and vulnerable sections of society and improve their social and economic security. This is done through accelerating the rate of GDP, implementational of policies for individual sectors for employment generation. The support oriented social security programmes concentrate on land reforms to help the poor, promotional security measures like EGS, JRY, IRDP, SGSY, basic needs like primary education, health, PDS, ICDS, reducing social exclusion etc. and protective social security measures to overcome contingent poverty, sickness, accidents, old age etc. In the security oriented social security policy experience of Kerala and Tamil Nadu is laudable and be implemented by other states in India. The impact of social security schemes depends upon effective implementation by government. The promotional and protective programmes will reach effectively to the poor depending upon decentralisation, access to information and social mobilisation.

The economic reforms, it is generally believed, will make the state withdraw from some of its economic activities. This proved correct. However states intervention is a must in the labour related activities, particularly affecting unorganised labour. As a proportion of GDP, the share of social sector expenditure has not increased during the reform period (first generation) except 1999-2000 in the total expenditure of Centre and States put together. There may be differences, ups and downs, in some years and in some states for eg. rich states like Goa, West Bengal spent more on social security programmes compared to poor states. Even in the latter the record of Bihar and UP is quite dismal. The expenditure on education (by central govt.) declined between 1990-99, except elementary education. Foreign aid was only limited to child labour. There has been under utilisation to the extent of 10% of plan expenditure. Compared to foreign countries, in the west, in Asial and to other developing countries, social sector expenditure in India is small.

The above analysis drives to one significant conclusion. The country like India can ill afford to reduce expenditure and in the tenth Five Year Plan Government of India should increase the allocation in every year budget. Thee is need for better and efficient utilisation of allotted money for social sector. The Planning Commission and GOI (2000) admit failures in the implementation (poor quality). The remedy lies in decentralisation, grass roots level vigilance, participatory approach by people, commitment by government officials and political power for helping the poor workers (both in organised and unorganised sectors) to over come deprivation and vulnerability so as to lead a better quality of life.

1. Beveridge Committee Report, 1942, p. 120.
2. International Labour Organisation Report, 1958, p. 11.
3. Ahmed E., Jean Dreze, J. Hills and A. Sen (1994): "Social Security in Developing Countries." Oxford University Press, Oxford.
4. Some parts and data in this section are taken from Mahendradev (2001).
5. Dreze Jean and A. Sen (1989) "Hunger and Public Action", Oxford, Clarondon Press, p. 1983.
6. C.P. Thakur and C.S. Venkataratnam (2001) "Social Security for Organised Labour" in Social and Economic Security in

India" ed. by S. Mahendradev and others Pub. by IFHD, New Delhi, p. 64.

7. Taken from Mahendradev (1999).
8. See the Union Budget for 2002-03.
9. Drawn from S. Mahendradev (Dec. 2001).
10. The Hindu, December 1, 2001, p. 10.

REFERENCES

1. Guhan S (1992): Social Security Initiatives in Tamil Nadu 1989, in S. Subramanian (ed.) Themes in Development Economics, Essays in honour of M. Adiseshaiah, Oxford University Press, Delhi.
2. Guhan, S (1993): "Social Security for the Poor in the Unorganised Sector: A Feasible Blueprint for India", (Eds.) Parikh K.S. and R. Sudarshan (1999).
3. Ginnekan W.V. (1998): "Social Security for all Indians" Oxford University press, New Delhi.
4. Prabhu Seetha (2001): Economic Reforms and Social Development, Sage Publications, New Delhi.
5. S. Mahendra Dev and Others (Eds.) 2001: Social and Economic Security in India: IFHD, New Delhi.
6. The Indian Journal of Labour Economics (2001), Conference Issue, No. 4, October-December.

2

IMPACT OF SOCIAL SECURITY INITIATIVES IN UNORGANISED SECTOR: THE CASE OF WOMEN BEEDI WORKERS IN RURAL AREAS OF TAMIL NADU

Velayutham Saravanan

The Problem

In Indian economy, about 90 per cent of the work force are in the unorganized sector despite low wages, uncertainty of employment and under-employment. They are deprived of benefits like provident fund, dearness allowance, wage for holidays, maternity benefits, credit facilities. Since Independence, the government has enacted several legislations to protect these workers and implemented various social security schemes for their betterment. The existing schemes are mostly confined to the providing old age pensions, maternity benefits and assistance to landless agricultural labourers and destitute women. However, the acts and the state-sponsored social security programmes have not produced the expected results in general and particularly among women in the unorganised sector. Under this situation, here an attempt has been made to analyse the impact of social security schemes for women beedi workers in the rural areas of Tamil Nadu.

Existing studies on the socio-economic conditions of beedi workers in the different parts of the country show their continuing struggle for survival while sustaining in this occupation despite low wage, irregular employment, and different forms exploitation by the middlemen and agents; lack of credit, education and medical facilities; and negligence in government policies (Ayachat 1978; Mishra 2000; Timir Basu 1978). Their condition has not improved in any remarkable manner, in spite of the many legislations and the efforts of trade unions.

There are several studies on the socio-economic conditions of Beedi workers and their problems in the different parts of the Indian sub-continent. A study (1974) shows that although the government had fixed the minimum wage for the Beedi workers, they never realized it and continued to be exploited by their employers. Though the minimum wages act provided for payment for weekly holidays; annual leave, maternity leave for the women workers, sick leave and medical benefits, the workers were yet to get these benefits. Further, they remain in a precarious situation where there is no job security. The Beedi manufacturers, by influencing the government, had prevented the implementation of the acts. The efforts of trade unions have proved to be unsuccessful. Timir Basu (1978) found that the condition of Beedi workers, already languishing in poverty, had further deteriorated due to rejection of Beedies, low wage rate and the clutches of moneylenders. Anil Avachat (1978) says that women Beedi workers were being exploited not only economically but also sexually. Since the Beedi manufacturers had political patronage, the role of the Labour Ministry/Department always remained ineffective. According to Mohandas (1980), a vast majority of the workers were not getting most of the benefits conferred by the different acts. The trade unions, plagued by lack of unity and disintegration, also remain powerless. Mohandas and Kumar (1992) found that both wage and non-wage benefits of the workers at the co-operative Beedi manufacturing units are much higher than those engaged in factory or house-based production.

At the regional level, there are several studies on Beedi workers in Tamil Nadu pertaining to the last decade, particularly about North Arcot district. These studies have focused mainly on the socio-ceonomic conditions, child labour and health problems etc., both in the rural and urban areas (Dominic Savio, 1991; Srinivasan, 1999; Duraimurugan, 2000; Thangaraju 1993; Vadamalai, 1990; Aarthi, 1999).

To eradicate these problems, the government has launched several social security measures and enacted several legislations to protect as well as promote them in recent years, particularly after 1970s. Given the scenario, the paper attempts to analyse the impact of social security initiatives for the Beedi workers in the rural areas, where diversified employment opportunities do not exist. It would interesting to know what are the existing social security schemes for the women Beedi workers. The extent of their awareness about these schemes and the benefits they have received could be probed into along with the problems and constraints they encounter in availing them?

The main objective of this article being a study of the impact of social security initiatives for women Beedi workers in the rural areas of Tamil Nadu, the erstwhile North Arcot district,[1] having the highest number of Beedi industries and workers involved in these activities had been selected for the purpose. According to the 1961 Census, the number of Beedi industries was high in the North Arcot district. There were 62 villages engaged in Beedi manufacturing activities in the district. Of them, one village viz., Katteri was selected for the study on the basis of highest concentration of Beedi industries and workers.

Katteri village is located at about 110 kilometers northwest of Vellore, the district headquarters, between Jolarpet and Tiruppattur towns. It is well connected by rail and road network. On the northern boundary of the village run the Chennai-Bangalore railway line and Tiruppattur-Kuppam road and in the southern boundary lay the Cochin-Chennai railway line and Salem-Chennai road. Katteri is spread over 3.5 kilometers and the people are living throughout the geographical areas of the village. There are seven hamlets viz., Indira Nagar Colony, K.R.S. Vattam, J.K.

Vattam, Lorry-shed, Muniyan Vattam, Bairavan Vattam and Pikkiri Thakka, besides the main village. Each hamlet is occupied predominantly by a particular community. For instance, Pakkiri Thakka is mostly inhabited by Muslims and Indira Nagar by *Dalits.* Further, within each hamlet, the settlements are again found to be scattered into groups of few houses and to some extent the people do reside in the farmlands. There are 807 households, of which, only 513 (64 per cent) are engaged in Beedi works and the rest 294 (36 per cent) are non-Beedi households. Beedi work is the main occupation for 508 (99 per cent) of the Beedi households while it remains a secondary occupation for the remaining 5 (1 per cent). Of the Beedi households, 100 have been taken for the intensive study.

The article consists of six sections. The second section analyses the growth of Beedi industries and changing mode of production. The third section discusses the role of trade unions in the evolution of the social security initiatives. The fourth section gives an account of the government policies and the various social security schemes being implemented for the Beedi workers, especially for the women in particular. The fifth section analyses the impact of the social security schemes and the last section ends with the concluding observations.

Growth and Changing Pattern of Beedi Industries

Historically, the economy of North Arcot district is predominantly dependent upon agricultural and allied activities besides silk-weaving and other traditional household activities. Of the traditional activities, Beedi manufacturing is a notable one. Initially, the Beedi industries were concentrated in Vellore and other towns, but later they had spread out to the rural areas of the district. Even in the rural areas, they are largely located at places adjoining the towns and cities. Although these industries are scattered over the different taluks, their concentration is confined to a few pockets like Gudiyatham, Tiruppattur and Vellore taluks. The 1961 Census has enlisted 707 Beedi industries in the district. Of them, 217 units (30.69 per cent) were located in the rural areas and the rest 490 (69.31 per cent) in the urban areas. Within the rural areas, little more than one-third of the Beedi units were housed in Tiruppattur followed by Gudiyatham and Vellore taluks. The rest of the taluks have only less then five per cent of the Beedi industries. Of the urban areas, the largest number of Beedi units were located in Vellore taluk which accounted 43 per cent, followed by Tiruppattur (24.33 per cent), Gudiyatham (17.54 per cent) and Walajapet (8.77 per cent). The remaining taluks have less than three per cent of the industries. It categorically shows that both in the rural and urban areas, the Beedi units are concentrated only in a few taluks. Thus the area of concentration is confined to Walajapet, Gidiyatham, Tiruppattur and Vellore taluks. Except Vellore town, the largest number of Beedi units are to be found both in the rural and urban areas of Tiruppattur taluk of North Arcot district, where the present study is undertaken.

Although only 9,846 workers were employed in the Beedi industries, a very large number of people, including leaves and tobacco vendors and those doing labeling, bundling, trade, business, besides other services are involved in this district. According to the 1961 Census, 28,231 workers were engaged in the Beedi related works, of whom, 24,367 were males and 3,864 females. Of the total workers, 18,635 were in the urban (15,461 males and 3,184 females) areas. There were 8,722 workers engaged in the household units (5,515 males and 3207 females) and 19,509 workers in the non-household industries etc., (18,852 males and 657 females). Further, the data evidences that the proportion of the female work force in the Beedi related industries is high in the allied works and very low in the non-household activities. In short, the rate of participation of women Beedi workers in the non-household industries is very low. Since we do not have the same data for the subsequent period, let us have a look at this trend in the study area where a large number of them are engaged in these activities.

Although Katteri is primarily dependent upon the

agrarian economy, Beedi rolling is a prominent occupation for a large number of households. Historically, though the Beedi industries have existed even during the pre-independence period, authentic data is available only since the 1960s. There were 20 Beedi industries in the village employing about 1000 people during the 1960s. But the nature of Beedi manufacturing then was totally distinct from that of the present. Earlier, manufacturing was held under the sheds and sub-centres of different brands of Beedi also existed. Under this system, a unit owner used to employ around 50 labourers, who were forced to work for long hours for very low wages. The shed-owner used to extend advances to keep the workers under their control and treated them as 'bonded'[2] labourers. This system was in vague till the mid 1980s.

(a) Changing Pattern of Beedi Industries

Initially, there were some trade unions in this village and the Beedi workers too actively participated in the union activities. But, later in the early 1980s, the trade union leaders/representatives had become subservient to the shed/Brand owners betraying the interest of the labourers. Consequently, the workers deserted the trade unions and started working with the owners as labourers. Even now, there is no trade union activity in this village. As mentioned earlier, some of the Brand Beedi branches/centers either closed their business or shifted to the other places. However, some units of the prominent brands viz., Mada Beedi, Coimbatore Beedi and KRS Beedi continued to their operations even now. Interestingly, these units are not engaged in direct manufacturing of Beedi under their own sheds or factories. At present, they are collecting the Beedis from the workers through agents and label them for sale under their own brand. Basically, the factories have ceased to be production centers as they are doing the labeling and packaging business, hardly employing any worker for Beedi rolling. This trend could be ascertained from the Census data.

(b) Changing nature of Occupation in Beedi Industries

Till 1980s, Beedi manufacturing was held at the factories/sheds in Katteri village. Then the proportion of the work force was high in non-household activities and low in household activities. Since 1980s, there was a steady reversal with the proportion of the work force in the household activities registering a remarkable increase (see Table 2.1). The continued operations of three sub-branches of Starch Beedis and Branch of Mangalore Ganesh Beedies in the mid-80s, employing around 200 workers in their factories was not without problems and tensions. Conflicts emerged between the workers and managers of the sub-branches over loans/chits extended to the workers and the quality of tobacco and leaves supplied for rolling. The managers' allegation was that the workers, who borrowed money or chit by assuring to return in weekly installments with interest, failed to repay in time and also sold the quality tobacco supplied to them or mixed inferior stuff. The refrain of the workers was that they were not given quality tobacco and leaves and were charged an exorbitant rate of interest for the borrowed amount. The signed 'chit' of a Branch manager is considered as 'currency' in the village. The worker could barter a chit from the Branch Manager for buying provisions and liquor within the village. Every week the Branch Manager would pay the money to whoever produced the chit. Further, the workers complained that they were being treated as bonded labour. According to the workers, the Branch Managers kept a watch on their movements. A visit to a movie hall would invite a warning. Consumption of liquor would be condemned. Consequently, the workers boycotted the work. Eventually, an agreement was reached between the workers and Branch Managers following the intervention of trade union leaders. However, Beedi rolling ultimately became a household activity in Katteri. The government's move to implement the Minimum Wages Act might have indirectly accentuated these changes.

TABLE 2.1
CHANGING OCCUPATIONAL PATTERN IN BEEDI INDUSTRY (HOUSEHOLD AND NON-HOUSEHOLD)

Year	*Total Main Workers*	*Total workers both in HHI & NHHI*	*Percentage of HHI & NHHI to MW*	*Total workers in HHI industries*	*Percentage of HHI industries to HHI & NHHI*	*Total workers in NHHI industries*	*Percentage of NHHI industries to HHI & NHHI*
1961	1,574	468	29.73	100	21.37	368	78.63
1971	1,448	533	36.81	16	3.00	517	97.00
1981	1,800	654	36.83	654	100	–	–
1991	2,079	1908	91.77	914	95.07	94	4.93

Source: District Census Handbook, North Arcot District (various Censuses)

Trade Unionism and Social Security Initiatives

The trade unions have played a prominent role in forcing the state to launch the social security measures for the labourers in the unorganized sector. Since Independence, the trade unions have strived to highlight the grievances of the workers in the unorganized sector in general and the Beedi workers in particular. They have been fighting for the protective and the promotion measures. Of course, the former would ensure the latter. Broadly, the protective measures for the women Beedi workers are: minimum wages act, pension, bonus, holidays payment and leave payment and the promotion measures' are: credits, hospitals, schools, scholarships, housing etc. The trade unions have represented these problems to the government in various forms—petitions, dialogues, *hartals* and processions—over the period. Let us see the role of trade unions in ensuring the proper implementation of the social security programmes in North Arcot district between 1970s and 2000s.

Since the middle of 1950s, the trade union movements, particularly those affiliated to the Communist Party, had represented the cause of Beedi workers to the government through petitions besides highlighting the issues through several forms of protests. As early as in 1956, when the trade unions activists held a protest demonstration in front of the Tamil Nadu State Assembly premises, several of them were arrested. In response to their demand, the Tamil Nadu Government had introduced the Madras Beedi Workers Act in 1958. Challenging this Act, the Beedi manufacturers filed a writ petition at the High Court of Madras. Until the early 1970s, there were only a few trade unions but their numbers have increased to more than 80 in 1998. In fact only 9 trade unions have taken up the issues concerning the Beedi workers of North Arcot district.

Since 1960s, the North Arcot District Beedi Workers Trade Unions and their Branches (predominantly Communist Party affiliated) have represented the Beedi Workers and raised various problems of the workers at different periods. These issues were settled with the Beedi Trade Mark Owners and Tobacco Merchants Association, Vellore, before the Commissioner of Labour, Chennai. The issues raised by the Beedi workers and those settled or remaining unsolved, and the emergence of the new problems over the period are given below:

Sl. No.	*Years*	*Issues Raised by the Trade Unions*	*Agreement Reached*	*Unsolved Issues*
1.	1972	(i) Assurance for 6 days work	Accepted	
		(ii) Weekly payment	Accepted	
		(iii) Demand for holiday wages	Accepted	
		(iv) Bonus for 1968-69 and 69-70	–	Unsolved
		(v) National and festival holidays	–	Unsolved
		(vi) Lay of compensation	–	Unsolved
2.	1974	(i) Revision of Wages	Accepted	
		(ii) Revision of Bonus	Accepted	
		(iii) Beedi Act should be implemented	Accepted	
		(iv) Dearness Allowance	Accepted	
		(v) Revision of Bonus Arrears	Accepted	
		(vi) Implementation of Holidays	Accepted	
		(vii) All other issues	–	Withdrawn
3.	1977	(i) Increase of Wages	Accepted	
		(ii) Increase of Bonus	Accepted	
		(iii) Implementation of Act	Accepted	

Cont.

Sl. No.	*Years*	*Issues Raised by the Trade Unions*	*Agreement Reached*	*Unsolved Issues*
		(iv) Welfare Amenities	Accepted	
		(v) One day wage for every 20 days of work	Accepted	
4.	1980	(i) Revised Wages	Accepted	
		(ii) Revised Bonus	Accepted	
		(iii) Provident Fund	Accepted	
		(iv) Supply of thread	Ensured	
		(v) Fall Back wages for six days' work	–	Not Accepted
		(vi) Agreement only for 2 years	Accepted	
		(vii) Other issues	–	
5.	1983	(i) Revision of wages	Accepted	
		(ii) Revision of Bonus	Accepted	
		(iii) Fall-Back Wages	–	Awaiting for Govt. decision
		(iv) Service card	Power given for enforcing authority	
		(v) Dearness allowance	Accepted	
		(vi) Other demands	–	Not Accepted
6.	1985	(i) Revision of Wages	Accepted	
		(ii) Revision of Bonus	Accepted	
		(iii) Other Demands	–	Unsolved
7.	1987	(i) Provident fund related issues	Accepted	
		(ii) Ensure 6 days work	–	Advised to discuss and finalise
		(iii) Inadequate Supply of leaves	–	
8.	1988	(i) Revision of Wages	Accepted	
		(ii) Revision of Bonus	Accepted	
		(iii) Correct Quantity of leaves	Accepted	
		(iv) Six days work in a week	–	Awaiting Govt. Decision
		(v) Information to deduct PF at log book	Accepted	
		(vi) Supply of thread	–	
		(vii) Other issues	–	

Cont.

Sl. No.	*Years*	*Issues Raised by the Trade Unions*	*Agreement Reached*	*Unsolved Issues*
9.	1990	(i) Revision of Wages	Accepted	
		(ii) Revision of Bonus	Accepted	
		(iii) Ensure correct Quantity of leaves		Referred to the Inspector
		(iv) Six days work		Awaiting Govt. decision
		(v) Other issues		Unsolved
10.	1992	(i) Revision of Wages	Accepted	
		(ii) Revision of Bonus	Accepted	
		(iii) Ensure of correct quantity of leaves	Accepted	
		(iv) Ensure of 6 days work		Referred to the Inspector
		(v) Weekly holidays		Waiting for Govt. decision
11.	1995	(i) Revision of Wages	Accepted	
		(ii) Revision of Dearness Allowance	Accepted	
		(iii) Revision of Bonus	Accepted	
		(iv) Six days work	Accepted	
		(v) Service cards		Unsolved
		(vi) Provident Fund		Unsolved
		(vii) Weekly holidays with wage		Unsolved
12.	1998	(i) Revision of Wages	Accepted	
		(ii) Revision of Bonus	Not Accepted	
		(iii) Revision of Dearness Allowance	Not Accepted	
		(iv) Other issues		Unresolved

Source: Memorandum of Settlement under Section 12(3) of the Industrial Dispute Act, 1947, Reached before the Special Deputy Commissioner of Labour, Chennai (Various years).

The trade unions have represented the grievance of the Beedi workers by submitting memoranda, appeals and call for bandhs besides taking up the legal avenue. Regarding bonus, the trade unions had filed cases at the Tamil Nadu Industrial Tribunal, High Court and Supreme Court in 1970s. Despite accepting the demands, the Beedi Owners have not implemented them. For example, regarding Provident Fund, an agreement was reached in 1987 itself to make the entry in the log book, including for women. In 1988, another agreement was made to furnish the full details of deductions. Although the Beedi owners had accepted this in principle, this was not implemented. Consequently, the same problems were raised time and again.

The wage rate fixed at different periods, based on the agreements reached between the representatives of the Trade unions and the Beedi Trade Mark Owners Association in the presence of the Director of the Labour Department, Chennai, are given in Table 2. In 1968, the wage rate for 1000 Beedies was Rs. 3.25. It increased gradually by 1992, hiked during 1998 and reached the highest rate between 1998 and 2001.

TABLE 2.2
WAGE RATES OF BEEDI WORKERS IN NORTH ARCOT DISTRICT 1968-2001 (IN RUPEES)

Sl. No.	*Year of Settlement*	*Wages for 1000 Beedies*	
		Sada Beedies	*Jadi Beedies*
1.	1968	3.25	3.50
2.	1970	3.25	3.50
3.	1972	4.05	4.30
4.	1974	4.50	4.75
5.	1977	5.25	5.50
6.	1980	5.75	6.00
7.	1982	7.00	7.20
8.	1983	7.80	8.00
9.	1985	9.30	9.50
10.	1988	11.05	11.25
11.	1990	13.05	13.25
12.	1992	16.05	16.25
13.	1993	24.70	24.90
14.	1995	27.65	27.90
15.	1998	31.20	31.40
16.	2001	62.04	62.04

Source: Memorandum of Settlement under Section 12(3) of the Industrial Dispute Act, 1947, Reached before the Special Deputy Commissioner of Labour, Chennai (Various years).

The trade unions have not only fought for increasing the wages but also took up different issues viz. six days work for a week, weekly payment of wages, wages for holidays/ festival holidays, weekly holidays, bonus, dearness allowance, provident fund, supply of thread and the shortage of leaves. Let us see the rate of bonus for the Beedi workers in the North Arcot district between 1974 and 2000. Till 1972 or until the intervention of the trade unions, no bonus was given. Until 1992, the bonus rate was very low, but it has increased remarkably in 2001 (Table 2.3).

TABLE 2.3
BONUS RATE FOR THE BEEDI WORKERS IN NORTH ARCOT DISTRICT (IN PAISE)

Sl. No.	*Year of settlement*	*Bonus for 1000 beedies*
1.	1968	–
2.	1970	–
3.	1972	–
4.	1974	20
5.	1977	25
6.	1980	35
7.	1983	50
8.	1985	60
9.	1988	80
10.	1990	110
11.	1992	150
12.	1995	232
13.	1998	262
14.	2001	444

Source: Memorandum of Settlement under Section 12(3) of the Industrial Dispute Act, 1947, reached before the Special Deputy Commissioner of Labour, Chennai (Various years).

However, most of the Beedi workers were not members of any trade unions, but they have initiated several demands to protect the Beedi workers, which reflected in government policies at the different periods of time.

Government Policies

The government policy consists of both enactment of act

and implementation of various schemes for women Beedi workers.

(a) Enactment of Acts

The problems of Beedi workers were not considered either by the colonial government or by the trade unions during the colonial period. While the same policy of non-intervention was followed by the government even after Independence. The trade unicn leadership too was insensitive to these issues, till the early 1970s. Initially, the Left parties launched the trade unions for the Beedi workers in North Arcot district and they were successful, because these industries operated at the factories. Since 1980s, the factory/shed type of industries have mostly collapsed with Beedi manufacturing becoming a household business. However, the trade unions continued to effectively highlighted the grievances of the Beedi workers in different forms. Responding to their demand, the government (Labour Department) conceded to convene a meeting between the trade union representatives and Beedi Manufacturers Association, once in two years. Even though the meetings were held regularly, the trade unions continue to represent their grievances to the government often. The representatives of the Beedi workers raised several demands like wage hike, bonus, weekly holidays with payment, pension, scholarship, medical facilities.

Although the government had initiated the dialogue between the Beedi Manufacturers and Beedi workers, it did not have any welfare policy/act for the upliftment of Beedi workers till the last quarter of the twentieth century. The government of India had enacted the Beedi Workers Welfare Cess Act 1976, Beedi Workers Welfare Fund Act 1976, Beedi Workers Welfare Cess Rules Act 1977 and Beedi Workers Welfare Funds Rules 1978. Similarly, the Tamil Nadu Government had enacted the Tamil Nadu Beedi and Cigar Workers (Conditions of Employment) Rules 1968, Child Labour (Prohibition and Regulation) Act 1986 and Child Labour (Prohibition and Regulation) Rules 1988. However, these acts had not produced the expected results for the Beedi workers in general and women in particular.

(b) Social Security Schemes for the Beedi Workers

In response to the demands from the trade unions and Beedi workers, the government has initiated several social security schemes and preferential treatment for the Beedi workers in general and women in particular. They are:

(A) **Health:** Static-cum-Mobile/Static Allopathic and Ayurvedic Dispensaries for Beedi workers; Scheme for reservation of beds in TB hospitals for Beedi workers; Scheme for Domiciliary Treatment of Beedi workers suffering from TB; Scheme for treatment of Beedi workers suffering from Cancer; Scheme for treatment of Beedi workers suffering from Mental Diseases; Scheme for treatment of Beedi workers suffering from Leprosy; Grant of financial assistance to Beedi workers for purchase of Spectacles; maternity benefit scheme for Female Beedi workers; Scheme for payment of Monetary compensation for sterilization of Beedi workers and Re-imbursement of expenditure as financial assistance to Beedi workers in respect of Kidney Transplantation.

(B) **Social Security:** Group Insurance scheme for Beedi workers.

(C) **Housing:** Build your own house scheme for Beedi workers; Housing scheme for economically weaker sections of Beedi workers; Grant of subsidy to Co-operative societies of Beedi Industries for construction of worksheds and godowns and group Housing for Beedi workers.

(D) **Education:** Award of scholarship to the children of Beedi workers; Composite scheme for financial assistance to the school going children of Beedi workers for supply of one set of dress, slates, note books and text books; Scheme to provide incentive/ financial assistance of Re. 1 to female children of Beedi workers, on the basis of attendance in schools.

(E) **Recreation:** Supply of T.V. Sets to the Beedi Workers by Industrial Co-operative Societies; and Establishment of community halls in Beedi Workers housing colonies with colour TV sets.[3]

Impact of Social Security Initiatives on Women Beedi Workers

This section analyses the impact of the social security initiatives for the women Beedi workers both in terms of protective and promotional measures in the North Arcot district.

(a) Wages

Apart from rolling Beedies, the women work as assistants/helpers to the main workers and are engaged in other Beedi related works like ring-making, leave-cutting, closing the Beedi ends and wage works. Out of the 100 women workers, 34 per cent are helpers/assistants; 16 ring-workers, one daily-wage worker and 43 Beedi workers, while 5 did not have work during the last week of the survey. The assistants do not get any wage and their productivity would be added to that of the main workers. The ring workers get wages on piece rate basis, which is not uniform. Suppose, if the worker himself collects the Beedies from the factory for labeling, he would get Rs. 3 per 1000 Beedies. If the worker collects through some one, he would get between Rs. 1.50 and Rs. 2 per 1000 Beedies. The leave-cutters and Beedi-end closers get daily wages. These kind of works would not involve any deduction.

Since the early 1970s, the government has fixed the minimum wages for rolling 1000 Beedis. But the Beedi workers never got the statutory wages from the owners or agents. The agents continue to exploit the Beedi workers in two ways: One, while supplying the raw materials i.e., leaves and tobacco to make 1000 Beedies, they always provided insufficient quantities to make the fixed quantity. Being forced by the agents to produce the fixed quantity of Beedies, they invariably purchased raw materials from the market to meet the scarcity. For this, the Beedi workers would have to spend from their own pockets. Unless they produced the fixed quantity, the agents, besides rejecting the finished products would refuse to make supplies in future. Second, while taking back the finished products they used to ask for more Beedies (i.e., for 1000 Beedies they used to demand 1100 Beedis) and would reject at least 100 Beedies, saying that the six and length do not conform to the expectations. In short, the Beedi workers were being forced to purchase on their own the raw materials to make up for the additional demand or else they would have to face rejection of the product.

Generally, the Beedi workers are not aware of the minimum wages act and their rights. Only 5 (12 per cent) of the women workers are aware of the minimum wages act and the others know nothing about it. According to the survey, 43 women workers are engaged in rolling Beedies. Of the women, except five all others (88 per cent) are ignorant of minimum wages. Except three woman workers, the remaining 40(93 per cent) complained about the contractors deducting their wages.

Invariably, most of the workers faced wage deduction for leaves, tobacco and size and length. According to the survey, 35 (88 per cent) of the women suffered wage deduction for the leaves, tobacco and size and length of Beedies. The deducted amount varies: 4 (11 per cent) up to Rs. 5; 12 (34 per cent) between Rs. 6 and Rs. 10; 6 (17 per cent) between Rs. 11-15 and 13 (37 per cent) more than 15 rupees for 1000 Beedies. The wages for four (10 per cent) workers was deducted only for the leaves, of which 2 (50 per cent) between Rs. 6-10 and the rest 50 per cent more than Rs. 11. One worker alone suffered deduction for upto Rs. 5 for size and length. Interestingly, none of them faced deduction for the tobacco. Except three women workers admitted that though they did not suffer any reduction, they received less than the statutory minimum wage rate. It shows that the deduction of wages is common in the Beedi occupation.

Due to huge deductions, the women Beedi workers of

TABLE 2.4
DETAILS OF THE AVERAGE WAGES

				Reasons for deduction per 1000 Beedies															*Net Wages per 1000 Beedies*			
				Leaves				*Tobacco*			*Size/length*			*All these three*								
Workers	*No*	*Knowledge on minimum wags act*	*Contractor deduct wages*	*No*	*Up to Rs. 5*	*6-10*	*11 & above*	*No*	*Up to 5*	*6 & above*	*No*	*Up to 5*	*6 & above*	*No*	*Up to 5*	*6-10*	*11-15*	*15 & above*	*Up-to 30*	*31-40*	*41-50*	*51-58*
Old	43	5	40	4	–	–	2	–	–	–	1	5	–	35	4	12	6	13	4	30	9	–

Source: Field Survey.

Katteri never realized the minimum wage rate fixed for 1000 Beedies. In the year 2000, the government fixed the minimum wage at Rs. 64.20 per 1000 Beedies. But the ground realities have not changed, for 4 workers (9 per cent) received only upto Rs. 30; 30(70 per cent) between Rs. 31-40 and 9(21 per cent) between Rs. 41-50 (Table 2.4).

(b) Other Benefits

Since Independence, particularly during the 1980s, several Acts were enacted to protect the Beedi workers from different forms of exploitation. In addition to that the government has implemented several schemes—pension, bonus, housing, medical facilities, scholarships for the children, maternity benefits—over the period. But only a very low proportion of the Beedi workers have availed these benefits. As per the survey, only 44 women workers were aware of the various welfare schemes. Even those who knew about the welfare measures have availed only limited benefits, mainly bonus. For instance, only 34 (77 per cent) of the 44 women who were aware of the schemes have received bonus, a nominal amount and not as prescribed by the Act (Table 2.5). The bonus was given either at the rate of Rs. 4 per 1000 Beedies or a saree and jacket annually. Two women workers had received provident funds and one availed maternity benefit. Four respondents have tried for scholarships but only two had received it. Very few respondents confirmed that they received the bonus and holidays pay together. Though nearly half of the

TABLE 2.5
DETAILS OF DIFFERENT BENEFITS AVAILED BY THE WORKERS

No. of House-holds	*Aware of the wel-fare mea-sures*	*Bonus*	*Provident Fund*	*Maternity benefits*	*Medical benefits*	*Scholar-ship*	*Hous-ing loan*
99	44	34	2	1	–	1	–

Source: Field Survey.

respondents were aware of different welfare measures, they could not claim their rights. Because once claims are made they would not get the raw materials.

(c) Health Conditions

Generally, back pain is common among the women Beedi workers who also face swelling of fingers and legs. Only 15 women (15 per cent) are free from health problems. According to the survey, 84 women workers suffer from one or the other form of health problems (Table 2.6). And back pain being the most prominent among them. Seventy-two women suffered from back pain and 16 have swelling of fingers and legs. Further, of the affected women, while 59 workers suffered regularly only 20 faced it occasionally. Although most of them are affected by different kinds of diseases, only 32 women workers were taking treatment while 50 have never taken any treatment. Most of them were being treated either at private or government hospitals. Except two respondents, none of them have ever visited the hospital for Beedi workers. Although the government has established hospital facilities for the Beedi workers they were not getting/taking the treatment due to their location and the time required for treatment.

TABLE 2.6
OCCUPATIONAL HEALTH OF BEEDI WORKERS

No. of House-holds	*Swelling of fingers*	*Deformity of fingers*	*Swelling of legs*	*Back pain*	*Cough/ wheez-ing*	*TB*	*Gyne-cological problems*	*Others*
84	16	4	13	72	–	3	2	13

Source: Field Survey.

(d) Awareness of the Beedi Workers

The Beedi workers are not aware of the social and political developments. According to the survey, a miniscule minority of 4 households of the women Beedi workers have some knowledge about these issues. Only one woman had got enrolled as a member of a political party while three others are associated with the social and cultural organizations (Table 2.7). No woman is a member of the panchayat, trade unions, NGOS and caste organizations.

TABLE 2.7
SOCIAL AND POLITICAL AWARENESS OF THE BEEDI WORKERS

	Members of					
No. of household	*Panchayat*	*Political party*	*Trade union*	*NGO*	*Social/cultural 1 org.*	*Caste Org.*
4	–	1	–	–	3	–

Source: Field Survey.

(e) Problems of the Beedi Workers

Till 1980s, the Beedi workers continued to work at the factories or sheds managed by the owner or branch manager. Supplied with leaves, tobacco and thread, they used to roll the Beedies under the direct supervision of the owners or Branch managers. They were exploited in different ways-being forced to work for more hours, compelled to produce more than 10 per cent of Beedies than the wages paid for, charged with high rate of interest for loans. In addition to that their movements during the rest of the day would also come under the watchful eyes of the Beedi owners. The labourers felt that they were being treated as slaves by the owners. But after the introduction of the Beedi Act, the Beedi Manufacturers had closed down the factories. Consequently, the factory system ceased to exist.

However, the factories and sub-branches continued to operate through the agents. The factories and Sub-Branches functioned merely as sellers of the raw materials and purchasers of the finished products. The agents play the role of a mediator between the owners and Beedi workers. They purchase the raw materials from the owners and distribute them to the workers. Then they collect finished products and handover them to the owners.

According to the survey, 66 (67 per cent) women are working with the contractors. Of them, 14 (2[illegible] per cent) have

TABLE 2.8
DETAILS OF THE CONTRACTING BEEDI WORKERS

No. of years working with the contractor									*Reasons for leaving*				
Up to 2	*3-5*	*6-10*	*11 & above*	*Log book & ID card*	*Loan from contractor*	*Contractor organized chit funds*	*If yes, you contributing*	*Earlier worked with other contractor*	*Closed down*	*Marriage*	*High rate of rejection*	*Insufficient supply*	*Others*
14	17	18	17	6	7	7	3	46	31	2	2	4	17

Source: Fied Survey.

been working for the last two years; 17 (26 per cent) 3-5 years; 18 (27 per cent) 6-10 years and 17 (26 per cent) more than a decade. Though most of the women workers are working with the contractors and they do not have any evidence to show that they are employed by the contractor. The survey reveals that only 6 (9 per cent) either have their names entereds into the log book or possess identity cards. It shows that the women workers are not being treated as a labour force officially and that their output is added to that of the male members of the household. Consequently, they are not entitled to avail the social security benefits, leading to further deterioration of their conditions. In other words, the productivity of the women Beedi workers is being undermined technical resulting in the denial of all statutory benefits in the rural areas.

The Beedi workers do change from one contractor to another for one reason or the other. According to the survey, 31 (47 per cent) of the women workers had worked with other contractors before being employed with the present contractors. Of them, 31 (67 per cent) have left the previous employer due to closure of factories; 2 (6 per cent) on account of marriage; 2 (6 per cent) because of high rejections; 4 (12 per cent) owing to insufficient work and the rest 7 (15 per cent) due to other reasons like migration, becoming a contractor themselves, etc Some of the respondents have shifted from 3-5 contractors. The data categorically shows that the Beedi workers, in spite of this shifting, remain under the grip of the contractors even though they are not technically under their control.

Conclusions and Policy Suggestions

In the unorganized sector, Beedi manufacturing provides huge employment opportunities, particularly for the women in Tamil Nadu. The government has enacted several Acts and implemented various kinds of social security schemes, including minimum wages, pensions, wage for holidays, medical facilities, shcolarships for their children, housing loan, dearness allowances, bonus for the Beedi workers in general and women in particular. But the benefits have not reached them. Because, most of the female workers do not have direct contact with the agents. Even if they had, they are unable to ascertain their rights, not only due to the ignorance about the available social security schemes, but also because of non-availability of other employment opportunities. Given the scenario, the following suggestions might be helpful for evolving appropriate policy initiatives.

Policy Suggestions

Based on the study the following suggestions are made for the policy initiatives for the Beedi workers:

(i) Existing 'contract'/'agent' system should be abolished. The contractors not only exploit the women Beedi workers by providing low wages and low quantity of raw materials but also the government social security initiatives.

(ii) All the workers those who associated with the different stages of Beedi works should be brought into account.

(iii) Beedi workers should be brought under the co-operative system at the village level so that every workers could be brought into account and avoid different forms of exploitation.

(iv) This form of arrangements not only helpful to the workers but also for the government to make appropriate policies.

REFERENCES

1. North Arcot district was bifurcated as Thiruvannamalai district and North-Arcot district during the 1980s.
2. The aged Beedi worker says that not only was the Beedi factory manager watching while working but they also watched their movements.
3. Ministry of Labour *Annual Report 1998-99*, Government of India.

BIBLIOGRAPHY

Avachat, Anil (1978) 'Beedi workers of Nipani' in *Economic and Political Weekly*, Vol. XIII, No. 29, pp. 1176-1178.

Avachat, Anil (1978) 'Beedi workers of Nipani' in *Economic and Political Weekly*, Vol. XIII, No. 30, pp. 1203-1205.

Census of India 1961 *District Census Handbook, North Arcot*, Vol. I and II.

Correspondent 'Maharasthra: Beedi workers of Sinnar' in *Economic and Political Weekly*, Vol. IX, No. 24, pp. 945-947.

Dharmalingam, D (1993) 'Female Beedi Workers in a South Indian Village' *Economic and Political Weekly*, Vol. XXVIII, Nos. 27-28, pp. 1461-1468.

Dominic Savio, K (1991) *Beedi Roling Child Workers*, (unpublished Project report) Tirupattur: Sacred Heart College.

Duraimurugan, B (2000) *A study on Child Labour in Beedi work at Tirupattur Town, Vellore District*, (unpublished Project Report), Tirupattur: Sacred Heart College).

Gopal, Meena (1999) 'Disempowered despite Wage Work: Women Workers in Beedi Industry' *Economic and Political Weekly*, Vol. XXXIV, Nos. 16-17, pp. WS-12-20.

Government of India *Beedi and Cigar Workers (Conditions of Employment) Act 1966*, New Delhi: Government of India.

Government of India *The Beedi Workers Welfare Cess Act, 1976.*

Government of India *The Beedi Workers Welfare Fund Act, 1976.*

Government of India *The Beedi Workers Welfare Cess Rules, 1977.*

Government of India *The Beedi Workers Welfare Fund Rules, 1978.*

Government of Tamil Nadu *The Tamil Nadu Beedi and Cigar Workers (Conditions of Employment) Rules, 1968.*

Government of Tamil Nadu *The Child Labour (Prohibition and Regulation) Act, 1986.*

Government of Tamil Nadu, *The Child Labour (Prohibition and Regulation) Rules, 1988.*

Government of India (1981) *Report on Working and Living Conditions of Workers in Bidi Industry*, Labour Bureau, Ministry of Labour.

Government of India (1994-95) *Report on Socio-Economic Conditions of Women Workers in Selected Beedi Units in India*, Ministry of Labour.

Mishra, Lakshmidar (2000) *Child Labourers in India*, New Delhi: Oxford University Press.

Mohandas, M (1980) 'Beedi workers in Kerala: Conditions of Life and Work' in *Economic and Political Weekly*, Vol. XV, No. 36, pp. 1517-1523.

Mohandas, M and Praveen Kumar, P.V. (1992) 'Impact of Co-operativisation on Working Conditions: Study of Beedi Industry in

Kerala' *Economic and Political Weekly*, Vol. XXVII, No. 26, pp. 1333-1338.

Srinivasan, R (1999) *Study on the problems faced by Beedi Rolling Workers*, (unpublished Project Report), Tirupattur: Sacred Heart College.

Tangaraju, N (1993) *The study of Socio-Economic conditions of Beedi workers at Pudukottai village, North Arcot Ambedkar Dt., Tamil Nadu*, (unpublished Project Report), Tirupattur: Sacred Heart College.

Timir Basu (1978) 'Beedi Workers of *Nippani' Economic and Political Weekly*, Vol. 13, No. 30, pp.

Vadamalai, L (1990) *A study of Socio-Economic conditions of Beedi Workers and their problems at Tirupattur, North Arcot Ambedkar District* (unpublished Project Report), Tirupattur: Sacred Heart College.

3

SOCIAL SECURITY FOR THE WORKERS IN THE INFORMAL CONSTRUCTION SECTOR

B. Vanitha

Provision for employment is advocated as a means for both poverty reduction and economic growth. The notion that well-being of individuals and households will be enhanced through he gaining of employment is often assumed rather than established. The straightforward link between work and well-being should be questioned especially in the case of effort intensive work. It is inappropriate to assume that enabling people to work will automatically enhance their well-being. A focus on employment in the Indian context most often means a focus on the informal labour market as the vast majority of Indians work in this sector which is associated with energy intensive manual labour. It is for this reason that an attempt is made in this paper to focus on the conditions and character of workers in the construction industry to illustrate how work may, or may not, lead to well-being.

Construction is an important sector of the economy contributing substantially to economic expansion and development. It is an integral part of every economic infrastructure like irrigation, energy, road transport and telecommunication. It is also a crucial component of social infrastructure like education, health, and shelter building and construction industry is a second largest economic activity in India next only to agriculture. It generates more incremental value added per unit of investment than any other industry. Calculations made with the input-output table relating to 1991-92 of the planning commission show that the construction sector has an output multiplier of 2 and an employment multiplier of about 5. Thus the backward and forward linkages of the construction sector makes it an important catalyst of growth and employment in the entire economy.

The construction industry has certain unique characteristics. Its products are customer designed ranging form small houses to big structures like dams and bridges. They are produced on site. The production process is slow and covers a wide spectrum of activities from highly labour intensive to the most capital intensive works. It is widely dispersed geographically and the activity is mobile in the sense that new works are initiated at another site after the work at one site gets completed. It makes use of a wide range of skills and expertise and a transient workforce. Employment in the industry is causal in nature and employment relations are generally not permanent. A substantial part of the construction workforce is therefore unorganized.

Employment in the construction sector is estimated to account for nearly 3.5 per cent of the workforce. Projections made by the National Institute for Construction Management and Research (NICMAR) show that employment in construction has expanded at a rate of 5% per cent per annum. The rate of growth of employment in construction is projected to increase to about 10.2 per cent per annum in 2004-05. Roughly about three fourths of the workforce are unskilled workers and about one seventh are skilled workers. Only one in twenty are technicians. The unskilled and skilled workers account for a substantial part of the workforce in construction and they consists of three segments namely,

1. Mandi
2. Institutional
3. Intermediaries

The first is the most informal and unorganized and it refers to the mass of people who assemble at market places in towns and cities for being hired by contractors and others requiring workers for construction work. The second is the workforce employed by construction companies engaged in contracting and government agencies. The last one is contract labour hired for work through intermediaries and sub-contractors.

In Coimbatore the prevalent system in respect of mandi workers is for them to line themselves up at some well-defined places form where the intending employer picks up the workers. Lack of employment opportunities is evident from the way they rush to the intending employers to pick them up for work. For the purpose of study 250 construction workers were selected at random and the required informations were collected through interviews scheduled in Coimbatore.

Out of the 250 workers selected 47 per cent is in the nature of sital who do the work of carrying of materials form one place to another, which requires minimum skill. 24 per cent is known as mamutial, who mix cement, 14 per cent of them are masons, who are expected to do the skilled job of laying bricks. There is 34 per cent of women workers, out of which 32 per cent is in sital category and 2 per cent in mamutial category. This evidences that women are generally engaged in less skilled jobs (Table 3.1).

With regard to their educational qualification, 37 per cent of workers are illiterates, 34 per cent of them are literate but without any formal education. 19 per cent of them have studied up to VIII standard and 10 per cent upto SSLC (Table 3.2).

For the same kind of job men and women workers are not being paid equally. For sital category of work the average wage paid to men is Rs. 90, while the women workers get just Rs. 60. This evidences that the women in the construction industry are mostly engaged in low paid jobs and there exists gender biased wage differentials (Table 3.3).

TABLE 3.1
DISTRIBUTION OF WORKERS AMONG VARIOUS CATEGORIES

Category of workers	*No. of women*	*No. of men*	*Total*
Sital	80 (32)	38 (15)	118 (47)
Mamutial	5 (2)	55 (22)	60 (24)
Mason	–	35 (14)	35 (14)
Plumber	–	15 (6)	15 (6)
Carpenter	–	22 (9)	22 (9)
Total	85 (34)	165 (66)	250 (100)

Figures in parenthesis indicate percentages of the column.

TABLE 3.2
EDUCATIONAL QUALIFICATION OF THE WORKERS

Educational Qualification	*Sital*	*Mamutial*	*Mason*	*Plumber*	*Carpenter*	*Total*
Illiterates	83 (33)	10 (4)	–	–	–	93 (37)
Literates with formal education	35 (14)	43 (17)	7 (3)	–	–	85 (34)
Std VIII	–	7 (3)	28 (11)	5 (2)	7 (3)	47 (19)
S.S.L.C.	–	–	–	10 (4)	15 (6)	25 (10)
Total	118 (47)	60 (24)	35 (14)	15 (6)	22 (9)	250 (100)

Figures in parenthesis indicate percentages of the column.

The common feature of diet of the workers is the inclusion of higher amount of cereals with low intake of protein rich food and protective food and the average calorie intake is estimated to be 2187 K.cal which much lesser than the recommended norms of around 3,500 K cal by ICMR (Table 3.4).

TABLE 3.3
AVERAGE WAGE PAID TO WORKERS

Category	*Average wage for men*	*Average wage for women*
Sital	90	60
Mamutial	120	90
Mason	150	–
Plumber	175	–
Carpenter	200	–

TABLE 3.4
CALORIE INTAKE OF WORKERS

Nutrients	*Percentage*
Carbohydrate	76.4
Protein	9.2
Fat	14.2
Total Calorie	**2187**

On an average the workers are engaged for nearly 20 to 22 days in a month and they work for nearly 10 to 11 hours in a day in the construction site, engaging in all types of construction activities.

TABLE 3.5
REPORTED HEALTH COMPLAINTS

Health complaints	*No. of Workers*	*Percentage of Workers*
Skin diseases	32	13
Fever, cough, eye sore	58	23
Asthma & breathing problems	35	14
Ulcer	10	4
Body pain and swatting	20	8
Cancer	–	–
Not affected	95	38
Total	**250**	**100**

62 per cent of the workers are aware of their health related problems. 13 per cent of them are suffering from skin

disease. 23 per cent of them are suffering from fever, cough. 14 per cent of the workers reported that they are suffering from breathing problems. 38 per cent of the workers are not affected by any kind of disease. It may also be possible that these workers are not aware of the sickness at all.

The health status of the workers has deteriorated due to occupational hazards and low calorie intake. Nearly, 42 per cent of workers in the sample have already met with minor work related accidents. Work in construction is highly accident prone. There are extensive safety guidelines and codes prescribed regarding operations such as excavation, blasting operations, erection of pre-fabricated parts, reinforced concreting. But the worker's primary concern is to earn money even at great personal risk as the work is seasonal in nature.

As far as their financial position is concerned, 91 per cent of the workers have no savings and 9 per cent of them have savings worth less than Rs. 5,000. Almost all of them have borrowed from outsides for higher rates of interest. 18 of them have their own house.

There are 89 children in the families of the sample workers, below the age group of 15 years, and most of them are engaged in some type of occupation. Sending the children to school is very difficult as these workers do not have a permanent place to work. Only 24 children are being sent to elementary school inspite of free education and noon-meal scheme.

Implications

Since the workers engaged in construction activities are scattered and fragmented it is very difficult to mobilize them and they are not amenable to unionization. The women are engaged in less skilled and low paid jobs and they have no access to skilled labour. There is also high level of insecurity. Though, since eighties, the participation of women in paid work has increased significantly there is no improvement in the quality of their employment interms of respect, dignity and equality. There is swelling of the informal sector with a corresponding increase in inequality, insecurity and suffering because of artificial integration of unevenly placed and developed regions (Rural and Urban). As a result the social costs in-terms of health, education, skills, capabilities and information are also increasing and highly prohibitive to common citizens.

Work related accidents and occupational diseases are also areas of major concern. Most of the accidents are man-made disasters arising form unsafe conduct. When accidents take place the affected worker do not get any compensation and has no means to subsist or sustain himself during the period of incapacitation. On account of working imbalances in income and employment opportunities between migrant sending and migrant receiving areas there is large-scale migration. The migrants are exploited, particularly women in low skilled occupations are cheated, denied of just, fair and equitable conditions of work.

Importance of Social Security and Protection

Social security is a multifaceted phenomenon and its importance has never been felt more acutely than now. It implies health, stable flow of income, access to public service, right to organize and defend one's rights etc. It is important that these measures are provided to the workers in the unorganized sector.

Social security for the unorganized sector is increasingly receiving the attention of academicians, policy makers, multilateral organizations and Non-Governmental organization (Breman J. 1996, Van Ginneken, 1997, 1998, Mahendra Dev 1999, Jhabvala and Subrahamanya 2000, Unni and Rani, 2001). The consensus in the literature is that the definition of social security needs to be broadened to encompass programmes that enables the individuals to attain a reasonable standard of living. Social security to the beneficiaries will add to the social product and also contribute to the wealth of the nation.

Social Security

More than 50 per cent of world's population is excluded today from any form of social security protection. Unequal access to labour market, increase in the informal sector activities due to displacement of modern jobs and insufficient capacity of the modern public and private sector to create new jobs has made the population to move in search of work in informal sector. This informal sector in-turn yields low income and low productivity. This prevents the people from realizing their potentials as workers and members of society. The insecurity breeds fear, impoverishment and socially irresponsible behaviour.

Collective Bargaining

It is absolutely necessary to provide institutional mechanism and procedure through which the voice of men and women at the workplace can be heard and their grievances are redressed. The freedom of association provides the basis for productivity and improved efficiency.

Basic Human Rights

There is also a need to recognize the basic human rights. Human capital included health, education and nutrition that are embodied in individuals and which translate into skills and abilities that are potential sources of labour managerial and entrepreneurial incomes. It is to be understood that we have no moral right or authority to deny the children their right to education and force them to work which is hazardous to their life.

Market forces cannot take care of basic human needs like education, primary health care, supply of water and environmental sanitation. We should promote opportunities for men and women to obtain decent and productive work. Not only the number of jobs created is important but more important is creation of jobs of acceptable quality.

There is also a need to develop a total gender perspective at the work place, so that women are entitled to justice and fair treatment in-terms of quality of access to employment opportunities and remuneration for work of equal value.

Quality of Life

The quality of life of the workers in the unorganized sector is very poor. Unplanned and unregulated urbanization has resulted in minimum civic facilities. Amenities like drainage, sewage, clean water and clean environment are very poor. The naked exposure to tons of dust and fumes emitted daily from the process of infrastructure development has also to be taken care of.

The diseases of poverty such as pulmonary tuberculosis and gastroenteritis reflect the poor living conditions along with lifestyle diseases like diabetes, hypertension etc. The government should on reducing the incidence of communicable diseases ensure that minimum levels of curative care reach the poorer sections of the population.

Social Protection Linked with Employment Policies

Contractual, casual and informal work have less secure forms of employment. Social protection through employee's provident fund, health insurance to these group of workers are also essential. The national social protection system which addresses the needs of women, casual labour, migrants, ethnic minorities, workers in the informal sector must be developed. Group insurance, housing schemes for economically weaker section of construction workers, financial assistance to school going children for supply of one set of dress, slate, notebooks and text books and award of scholarship to children may be introduced.

Conclusion

We cannot make our workforce be it in formal or informal sector competitive and productive unless it is literate, skilled, healthy and contended, motivated and stable. If the core labour standards are not observed and their basic rights are continued to be violated we cannot achieve a competitive, committed and productive workforce.

We cannot afford to depress their wages which would mean low calorie intake, low level of nutrition and low productivity. We need to develop strategic and comprehensive labour policy suited to the specific needs of the informal sector to solve the problems of poverty, unemployment and inequality. The well-being of individuals and households cannot be enhanced by early providing opportunities of employment but it must be associated with measures of social security.

With the introduction of economic reforms, India has been largely reduced to its business people who can export goods and services to other countries. Its women, children, peasants, workers and their basic rights are all disappearing. The camps of labour and capital are in conflict, but we cannot afford to let the labour lose the battle.

REFERENCES

1. Banerjee, N. (1985) Women workers in the unorganized sector. Sangam Books, Hyderabad.
2. Breman, J. (1996) Footloose labour: Working in India's informal economy, Cambridge University Press, Cambridge.
3. Dutta, R.C. (1999) "Public Action, Social security and unorganized sector". Paper presented at the conference on social security in India, Institute for Human Development, April 15-17, New Delhi.
4. Guhan, S. (1994) "Social Security options for developing countries", International Labour Review, Vol., 133. No. 1, Geneva.
5. Jhabvala, R. and R.K.A. Subramanya (2000) (eds). The unorganized sector; Work security and social protection, Sage Publications, New Delhi.
6. Mahendra Dev, S. (1999), "Social security in India—An overview of performance and issues". Paper presented at the conference on social security in India, Institute of Human Development, April 15-17, New Delhi.
7. Seetha Prabha, K. (2001) Socio-Economic security in the context of pervasive poverty: A case study of India, ILO, In focus programme on Social-Economic security May (mimeo).
8. Van Ginneken, W. (1997) "Social security for the informal sector: Investigating the feasibility of Pilot projects in Benin, India, BI. Salvadar and Tanzania" Issues in social protection, Discussion paper No. 5, ILO, Geneva.

4

SOCIAL SECURITY FOR WORKERS IN THE UNORGANISED SECTOR

Jayashree Dam P. Choudhary

Introduction

The unorganized sector and informal sector are two interchangeably used terms because of microscopic difference in their meaning. The "Central statistical Organizaion" (CSO) prefers using term unorganized sector, while "International labour Organization" (ILO) for the first time used term informal sector in 1972 when mission under UNDP was sent to Kenya to study employment and income situation of urban Ghana. Ordinarily the units not registered under Factories Act 1948 belong to unorganized sector, as such, they are called unprotected/unregulated sector, and to give better picture of situation all the terms are clubbed together under the banner of *"informal sector"*. This sector drew attention form early 1970s, as urban economics of the Third World countries failed to provide shelter to rising population in formal sector. Characteristically unorganized and informal sector are symmetrical but later is more holistic in approach. So during the process of discussion the terms alternatively may be used, as watertight analysis is not possible all the time.

The chosen topic ejects enough curiosity in the minds of academicians that there might be some inherent weakness of the sector for which workers are to be brought under the protection of social security measures. Moreover it leads to further clue that there is sector like "organized" which provides security under well-formulated monitoring body, and thus workers are well protected.

Distinction between Formal and Informal Sectors

To find out solution to inquisitiveness first it will be appropriate to draw distinction between formal and informal sectors on the basis of ILO guidelines and then to proceed towards desired goal to minimize the suffering of workers of unorganized sector. Quoting ILO's report on Columbia (1970) and Kenya (1972) from Mitra (1994) the following are the characteristics of informal sector.[1]

(i) Conditions of free entry into the product market.
(ii) Dependence on traditional resources.
(iii) Family ownership of enterprises.
(iv) Small-scale operation.
(v) Adoption of labour intensive technology.
(vi) Skill acquired outside the formal school system.
(vii) Unregulated and competitive markets (including the labour market).

On the other hand formal sector enjoys following advantages against the above-mentioned points.[2]

(i) Government protection.
(ii) Easy access to infrastructural facilities, bank finance, organized capital market, foreign technology and etc.
(iii) Highly unionized labour market.
(iv) High capital intensity.

The organized sector by virtue of its merits receives tenderly affection of government as a sign of economic development. This adversely reflects government's attitude toward unorganized sector while it acts as sponge by absorbing greater number of people both in wage-employments groups. The different research scholars through their empirical studies find strong linkages between formal and informal sectors; but when benefits are considered and found to be only restricted to workers of organized sector, then critics may term it as step-motherly attitude which should not happen in a developing economy, like India. For example, the group insurance scheme a common term in organized sector is launched on June 30, 2001 for agricultural workers whose share accounts for small percentage of unorganized sector. As a trial 20,000 agricultural workers in 50 blocks of 50 districts will be selected and first beneficiaries will be landless workers followed by marginal formers. India being an agricultural country, such steps would have been taken long back in order to reduce level of poverty and inequality between urban and rural people. There may be many packages for agricultural and allied activities but they fall to bring satisfactory result as 46% (HRD 1999) people still line below poverty line (BPL).

Reasons behind Growth of Unorganized Sector

The "unorganized sector" is divided in two categories (i) urban unorganized sector and (ii) rural unorganized sector. Here discussion will be carried on workers of urban unorganized sector however, journey will start with rural economy as chronic problems found in this area are responsible for large scale rural-urban migration, which in turn aggravates urban problems.

Rural unorganized sector

Agriculture is the mother occupation since time immemorial. Over the centuries keeping pace with time "industry" in some of the countries captured position of agriculture because of their superiority in technology, skill and knowledge, which paved journey towards advancement. In due course of time, Industrial development further helped those countries to enjoy status of "developed countries" and rest came to be known as underdeveloped countries. In between these two extremes are developing countries who are striving to become more prosperous in due time. Thus less developed countries are still agricultural countries, though dependency on this sector is gradually reducing. The most striving feature of this sector is that it does not enjoy status of industry till date, which other way could bring economic prosperity among the agricultural workers and marginal workers. The workers in this sector do all types of works where as industrial workers are engaged in specialized works.

The critical estimation of Indian planning of last five decades fails to justify its achievement in term of rural upliftment where agriculture is way to life. The disintegration among the agricultural workers has helped this sector to remain unorganized and continue to live within vicious circle of poverty. There may be some variation but when general condition is static then alternative means of livelihood to be found for survival, and probably with this motive rural people migrate to urban areas to join struggle of existence with urban unemployment. Here, it will be out of way to discuss about causes of fall of agricultural production; simply it can be said that natural factors and declining trend in crop production due to fragmentation are mainly responsible for rural-urban migration at large-scale (though current census report indicates falling rate of rural-urban migration but it does not effect present discussion as migrated people already have created problem for urban labour market).

Urban unorganized sector

Apart from rural-urban migration, inter/intra state migration, natural growth rate of population and immigration are responsible for fast growth of urban unorganized or informal sector. With the increasing problem of unemployment specially after globalization unemployment situation has deteriorated as theme of NEP (1991) is "produce or perish". Closing down of many industrial units specially the "textile industry" has further aggravated situation along with VRS, adopted by government to reduce size of local public sector enterprises. The present jobless growth budget of 2001-2002 is also just like adding salt to injury. With the closure of large number of industries million of workers were thrown to unemployment pool. Employment analysis records a growth of 2.1% in 1992-93 and 1.8% in 1993-94 and over the period

1992-97. 35 million additional job will be needed, 36 million for 1997-2002 while backlog of unemployment was 23 million in 1992. So projected estimate is 94 million of additional job 2002. Moreover the Union Budget 2001-2002 clearly mentions about reduction of size of government offices @ 2% per annum which for a period of next five years will lower down employment opportunity to 10%. Under such backdrop it can well imagine that urban unorganized sector will further become bulky in order to absorb the army of unemployment.

As the name suggests, people of this sector are to be engaged in micro enterprises, which are not mostly registered. To measure the magnitude of importance of unorganized sector it will be appropriate to quote from 51st round (July 1994-June 1995 NSS) report.

"The unorganized sector holds the key to understanding the economic situation in developing countries such as India. The importance of this sector had been by the Indian planners and policy makers in the 1950s. The need for statistical information about it was also widely recognized..."

(Introduction: 1.0)

In a developing economy, where population is high, quality of human resources is poor technological and capitals are obstacles on the way to industrial development, unorganized sector is panacea to solve problems temporarily arising out of these obstacles. Even in developed countries, the importance of the sector is recognized as they also face unemployment problem, which may be transitory for some of them.

The inherent characteristics of the sector have also tremendously helped towards the growth of urban informal sector in recent time. Where no norm is laid down for entry an illiterate, unskilled person according to suitability can find out occupation for survival. Probably because of such flexibility number of course reason is different with self-employeds.

Depending on types of establishments, NSSO categorized them into (i) Own account enterprises (OAEs) (ii) Non-

Directory establishments (NDEs) and (iii) Directory establishments (DEs).

However, enterprises under Factories Act 1948 employing 10 workers with power or more than 20 workers without power were beyond the purview of 51st round survey of unorganized sector.

Given such profile by NSSO, and ILO the conceptual framework of unorganized sector can easily be formulated. Taking all the factors into consideration including animate and inanimate resources of the developing economics, the unorganized sector is strong enough to accelerate process of economic development.

While policy makers are conscious about its economic contribution (60% in case of India) it will be justified to peep into benefits the workers are likely to enjoy during the tenure of their employment.

Empirical Testing on Guwahati Urban Market

Unlike other states of India, Assam is both agriculturally and industrially a backward state. As a result of this, growth of urban informal market has become spontaneous to accommodate displaced agricultural workers due to divesting flood and irregular earning due to single cropping system (in limited cases it is double cropping), cross border immigration, inter-state migration, urbanization and government policy to have reduced job opportunities in organized sector, etc. have rather created mounting unemployment problem for urban Guwahati.

Guwahati, being gateway to north Eastern Region, has become busy city in comparison to other state capital towns of NER. With the increased importance (From commercial point of view Tinsukia is nerve-centre of trade and commerce in Assam) of the city because of better infrastructural facilities, growth of shops, repairing centres, small establishment motor garage, grocery shops, tailoring, fast food and many other commercial establishments have come into existence. The increased number of commercial complexes with modern get up reflects changing standard of living of Guwahati dwellers, which was absent even few years back.

Keeping pace with time as numbers of automobiles have gone up, number of motor garages and scooter repairing houses have also gone up. So to match the topic few such establishment (Des) were selected for simple random sampling where young boys including child labour are engaged to carry on day to day struggle for existence.

From two garages altogether six persons were interviewed excluding the owners. The child worker (Ramie) was engaged in minor work @ 25 p/d and assisted the adult workers according to requirement. Before joining present work he worked as waiter in a hotel but left the place out of disgust. In present occupation also he was unhappy, as monthly payment was irregular. Extreme poverty had forced him to join labour market at a tender age, though he would like to enjoy childhood like normal children. He worked for daily 9-10 hours with a break of one (sometime it is less) hour for mid day meal. The owner provided tea to him along with other workers.

The other experienced workers would get in between Rs. 1200-2300 as per contract, but the biggest problem was that neither the amount would be paid in time nor in full. As a result of this hardly and workers in owned garage would continue for longer period. They would privately worked elsewhere to earn extra-money and there seemed to be hide and seek practice between employer and employees. The workers after attaining experience at particular place normally get better offer, so they need not sit idle and become absorbed by new employer soon. During casual interaction with garage workers it was clear that lack of trust and honesty on the part of employer are mainly responsible for workers to adopt unfair means at their work place. If payment of salary would have been regular, and better working condition could be overcome.

In garage "y" two underage boys were found working without any remuneration in monetary term. They were simply provided meals and tea by the owner since they were trainees. They were not in position to bargain but secretly earned pocket money by doing minor repairing work in the absence of the owner. Those who were engaged in welding or electrical works and for a long were attached with same employer their monthly income is around Rs. 3,000. They would get fringe benefits from time to time. But it happens in limited cases only where employer feels his workers are reliable, efficient and thus indispensable.

Generally workers of such segment of unorganized sector highly suffer from wage/salary insecurity, exploited by employers and to overcome because problem whenever they find better monetary offer they leave old working place. With increased number of vehicles there seems to be mushroom growth of garages as such there is demand for trained workers. While some are engaged in all types of vehicle related activities, some are specialized and even some will deal with brand names i.e., 'Maruti', 'Daewoo' and etc.

In following table workers qualification, experience, wage/salary etc are shown in order to assess their position in urban labour market of Guwahati:

TABLE 4.1
DIRECTORY ENTERPRISES IN UNORGANIZED SECTOR

No. of workers	*Sex*	*Status*	*Age*	*Qualification*	*Duration*	*Wage/ salary*	*Fringe benefits*
1.	M	Trainee	12 yrs.	Nil	3 months	–	Meals & tea
2.	M	Trainee	15 yrs.	II	6 months	–	Meals & tea
3.	M	Full time Worker (skilled)	22 yrs.	VI	2 years	1800/-	Not regular
4.	M	Un-skilled	14 yrs.	Nil	1 years	25/- p/d	(Nil)
5.	M	Skilled worker	24 yrs.	VIII	3 years	2200/-	During puja and Bihu
6.	M	Semi skilled	21 yrs.	IV	2 years	1200/-	

Source: Field survey.

Likewise four samples were collected from own account enterprise and establishment where condition of hired worker under establishment was found to be same as counterparts working in other segments of unorganized sector. The hired worker in establishment were better in turn of salary as it is regular in addition to fringe benefits. But if the employer is dissatisfied the workers can be removed immediately. So they suffer mainly from job-insecurity. The owner under (OAE) manages business at his best possible capacity. As he was reluctant to reveal his actual financial (he did not disclose even initial amount of capital investment) condition many of the questions remained unreplied.

TABLE 4.2
WORKERS OF OAE AND ENTERPRISE

No. of workers	*Status of workers*	*Age*	*Sex*	*Quali-fication*	*Salary (Rs.)*	*Experi-ence*	*Fringe benefits*
1.	OAE	45	M	B.A	10,000	6 years	–
2.	OAE	54	F	B.A.	6,000	2 years	–
3.	Enter-prise	23	M	B.A.	4,000	4 years	Medical benefits in case of need
4.	Enter-prise	19	M	H.S.	2,000	6 months	Puja benefits

In another field-survey simple or unrestricted random sampling technique was adopted and accordingly information about sample-size is furnished herewith:

From the given table it was clear that since last categories belonged to "child-labour" group, they did not have control over their income; they were engaged in economic activity out of extreme family poverty. Interpreting the table in statistical language it was found that saving(s) and expenditure (E) were of high degree of negative correlation, depicted in following scatter-diagram.

TABLE 4.3
WORKERS OF UNORGANIZED SECTOR IN GREATER GUWAHATI

Sl. No.	Types of activity	Sex	Age	Marital status	Level of education	No of children	Monthly/perday income	Monthly saving (Rs.)
1.	Idol maker	M	45	M	H.S.L.	2	Rs. 8,000 (average)	2,000
2.	Idol maker	M	35	UM	B.A.	–	Rs. 9,000	2,500
3.	Potter	M	28	UM	IV	–	Rs. 4000	800
4.	Rickshaw puller	M	28	M	III	3	Rs. 70 p/d.	500
5.	Rickshaw puller	M	38	M	B.A.	4	Rs. 70 p/d.	500
6.	Vegetable Seller	M	50	M	II	4	Rs. 300 p/d.	3,000
7.	Construction worker	M	35	M	I	3	Rs. 100 p/d.	700
8.	Construction worker	F	33	M	I	3	Rs. 60 p/d.	400
9.	Construction worker	F	17	UM	–	–	Rs. 50 p/d.	400
10.	Hawker	M	40	M	VI	4	Rs. 150 p/d.	800
11.	Hawker	F	35	M	II	3	Rs. 60 p/d.	300
12.	Panshop	M	26	UM	V	–	Rs. 300 p/d.	1,000
13.	Panshop	F	30	M	II	2	Rs. 100 p/d.	400
14.	Nut seller	F	35	M	III	3	Rs. 200 p/d.	1,000
15.	Juice seller	M	27	M	IV	2	Rs. 400 p/d.	2,500
16.	Juice seller	M	32	M	II	3	Rs. 200 p/d.	1,000
17.	Fish seller	M	34	M	I	4	Rs. 800 p/d.	3,000
18.	Fish seller	F	50	M	–	4	Rs. 600 p/d.	3,000
19.	Rag picker	F	14	UM	–	–	Rs. 20 p/d.	–
20.	Rag picker	M	12	UM	–	–	Rs. 25 p/d.	–

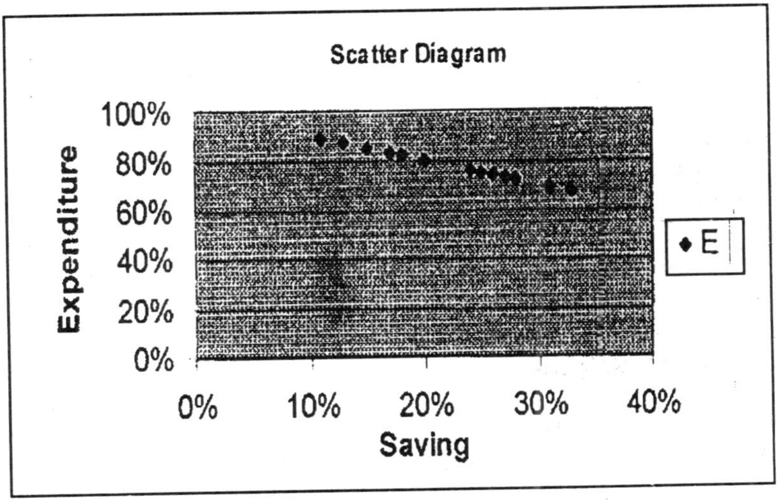

At this point one may argue that under normal condition relationship between saving and expenditure is always negative but in case of workers of unorganized workers situation is different when one talks in absolute term.

In this case state government with the help of financial institutions can rise living condition of workers whose "power to save" and "will to save" will go up in long run and it will ultimately help increase size of domestic capital

Considering their background and working condition variables it is need of the hour that social and economic securities are ensured to them at the earliest for smooth running of state economy and to realize objective of "growth with equality".

Necessary to Introduce Social Security Scheme for Workers of Urban Unorganized Sector

On the basis of above given tables it seems necessary to introduce social security schemes for workers of the unorganized sector, as underlying principle of policy is to ensure minimum standard of material welfare to all its citizens on a basis wide enough to cover all the contingencies of life from womb to tomb." The principle of social security discussed in different publications help draw inference that whole gamuf of concept is based on human-dignity-essence of human right and social justice.

In unorganized sector as no stress is given on quality of human capital, so other than OAEs the workers are mostly exploited by the employer both in term of wage and employment. The women and children who constitute major portion of unorganized workers are highly exploited because of their ignorance, unskilled ness and lack of awareness. Rather specifying any targeted group, on the basis of collected samples it can strongly be said that social security scheme should be introduced in this neglected sector as done in case of organized sector. While all categories of workers work not less than 9 hours p/d against all odds, uncertainties and hazardous works will not be social justice to ensure them two full squares of meals in return? The monthly wage range from Rs. 1200-Rs. 4000 (excluding OAEs) is even insufficient to maintain simple life in city like Guwahati (considered to be costly city in India) according to one's expectation. Considering the ages it may be assumed that as "single person" somehow they can pull on lives, but there is probability of having dependents. So if this is the situation how can they expect to enjoy quality of life in their personal lives?

There are different social security schemes that may be introduced in phased manner as recently done in West Bengal. Introduction of any of the schemes specially for urban unorganized sector workers of Guwahati labour market will bring qualitative change in attitude of both employer and employees.

Provisions under Social Security Scheme and Limitations of Government

The social security measures can broadly divided into two parts (a) Statutory and (b) non-statutory. There is in fact no separate provision for workers of unorganized sector in broader sense; so schemes introduced in case of workers of organized sector can easily be extended in case of such workers for upliftment of their socio economic condition. Moreover, with the given welfare-state concept combined with constitutional provisions one has right to live with dignity deprivation of which means violation of human rights. So whether the person is employed or unemployed it is the responsibility of state government to provide him with basic amenities, through social security measures.

Statutory provisions

The workers of unorganized sector are entitled to enjoy following benefits as per existing provisions of social security measures.***

1. The women's compensation Act 1923.
2. Maternity Benefit Act 1961.
3. The Employees State Insurance Act, 1948.
4. The Employees Provident Fund Act. 1952.
5. The Employees Provident Fund Act. 1966.
6. The Payment of Gratuity Act, 1972.

With the changes of time, significance of social security is more exposed of than before but due to financial constraints on the part of state government its operation largely has remained limited in organized sector only. To add lack of awareness, literacy, skill and process of recruitment are also responsible because of which workers of unorganized sector have failed to draw attention of appropriate authority. Disintegration among them has put themselves in disadvantageous position to bargain.

No doubt government form time to time has introduced different economic packages for economically weaker section of society living both in urban and rural areas (EAS, PMRY, SGSY etc) but because of bureaucratic process and lack of transparency desired level of achievement could not be reached.

In the present discussion while emphasis is given on workers of urban unorganized sector, so for them group

***Labour..... p. 335.

insurance scheme under social security fund plan of LIC can be introduced by the state government as done by Centre for agricultural workers in recent time. Under the provision the workers, irrespective of their types of establishment, (commercial, manufacturing, construction etc) may be brought under same umbrella and in a phased manner depending on situation on priority basis other provision can be introduced for overall development of the society.

The only capital the state government and Centre is the goodwill, honesty and dedication. In underdeveloped countries financial hardship will always persist, but through better management of resources the fund problem can be overcome.

Non-statutory provisions

As higher per cent of poor people live in rural areas, for them both statutory and non-statutory provisions of social welfare measures must run parallely. Probably with this perception govt. launched "Health for all", "Education for all", and "Food for all" programmes from time to time. It is only few back present Prime Minister declared his government's commitment to make India "Hunger free". The new scheme "Sampoorn Grameen Rojgar Yojana" ensures "food security" and "employment generation" in rural areas and if the entrusted machineries work with transparency it will open new vista for socio-economic development of the country.

The non-statutory provisions are enshrined in the concept of welfare state, so how far the state in question is committed to realize dream, will be reflected in how far government is successful to reduce gap between haves and have-nots. The sooner it is implemented the better for her to accelerate economic growth rate. Very recently it is appreciated by policy makers and economists that current slash-down of Indian economy is not because of low rate of inflation but of outstanding problems like poverty and social imbalances. So, if the present governments, both at state and central level, want to avoid doubtfulness, the social security measures are to implemented both for urban and rural workers of unorganized sector at the earliest.

Suggestions and Conclusions

There is a saying that "If you are hungry, you are to express your hunger", so unless the urban workers of unorganized sector ventilate their grievances in unionized form, no governments of their own accord introduce any scheme voluntarily. The case of agricultural workers is different as they are backbone of Indian economy. Introduction of social security schemes for rural workers specially, agriculture and its related activities may be due to plan provision and sometimes may be for sporadic reason, but village workers as a whole will enjoy some sort of benefits through different rural economic packages. But the case is different for urban workers. Here getting of engagement is easy but the question is whether they are in position to maintain minimum standard of living? Except the self-employment group, others cannot think of decent standard of living. So in order to live within framework of human rights, (i) the workers must be united irrespective of gender to draw attention of government and (ii) the government should recognize their contribution by providing social security at the earliest.

Introduction of such noble ideas will definitely increase standard of living of working class, minimize poverty and help realize socialism the inherent feature of constitution in long run.

N.B: 1. In case of tables 1 and 2 no statistical tool was used due to inadequacy of data.

2. From table 3 only 18 were included for analysis purpose since child-labour couldn't furnish their saving position.

REFERENCES

1. Mitra, p. 72.
2. Mitra, p. 76

Gupta K.R. (1997) Liberalization & globalizaiton of Indian economy.

Mitra Arup (1994) Urbanization, slums, informal sector employment and poverty (An exploratory study).

Mehorotra S.N. (1964) Labour problems in India. Competition Success Review, Apr. 2001.

NSS 51st round......

The Assam Tribune Sept. 11, 2001.

5

SOCIAL SECURITY FOR RURAL LABOUR: EXISTING PROVISIONS AND INSTITUTIONAL ARRANGEMENT

S. P. Singh

Introduction

Poverty and deprivation is not evenly spread among the all regions and all sections of society. Rural workers, especially marginal farmers and agricultural labourers, casual and contact labourers, child and women labourers and those without regular jobs are more prone to deprivation and vulnerability to deprivation. Rural workers of those regions[1], which are more sensitive to droughts, floods and other natural hazards, have higher risk of losing their lives and livelihoods. Rural labourers suffer from seasonal unemployment, job insecurity, poverty, indebtedness, bondage, migration, inability to get statutory minimum wages; illiteracy, mal-nourishment, lack of access to assets like cultivated land, discrimination, and incapability to form organisation. They do not have fixed employer-employees relation as most of them work either as casual labourers or as contact labourers and hence could not be entitled for all the protective social security benefits, which their counterparts get in organised sector. The process of macro economic contraction (e.g. lower public sector investment in farm and social sectors) and reduction in developmental role of the state, initiated during 1991 and thereafter, have actually worsened their economic condition. The quantitative restrictions lifted from agricultural products and attempt to dismantle PDS may put adverse impact on agricultural growth, which can result in reducing labour demand and hence further deterioration in the condition of rural labour. Therefore, to protect these poor workers from personal and covariate risks and to improve their living standard, there is a need to develop effective social security programmes and institutional arrangement to execute these programmes.

Keeping in view the above facts, this paper examines the existing social security measures for rural labour and suggests an institutional arrangement for conceptualisation, implementation and monitoring of various promotional and protective social security programmes. The paper has been organised in five sections including the introductory remarks made just now. The next section deals with the concept of social security in context of developing countries. The existing social security schemes for rural poor workers are examined in part III. An institutional arrangement for implementation of various social security programmes has been discussed in section IV followed by concluding remarks in the end.

Concept of Social Security

Social security is the security, which a society/state as a whole provides to its members against the common risks of life such as employment injury, disablement, diseases, old age, widowhood, unemployment etc. ILO (1984) defines social security:

> *"... the protection which society provides for its members, through a series of public measures, against the economic and social distress that otherwise would be caused by the stoppage or substantial reduction of earnings resulting from sickness, maternity, employment injury, unemployment, invalidity, old age and death; the provision of medical care; and the provision of subsidies for families with children."*

This definition is too narrow to be accepted in context of developing countries as it considers only the protective social security measures, while the promotional measures are equally important in developing countries. Three points emanate from this definition: First, social security has to be organised largely by the state and/or public institutions. Second, the definition presumes that the members of the society have already reached an acceptable standard of living and therefore, social security is to protect members of the society from any fall in their living standards'. Third, this definition refers to the risks, which are due to personal circumstances such as illness, death of main bread earner etc. (Jutting, 1999). It does not cover the risks, which occur due to fluctuations in the social surroundings particularly natural disasters such as droughts, earthquakes, floods etc.

According to Dreze and Sen (1991), *"... the basic idea of social security is to use social means to prevent deprivation, and vulnerability to deprivation."* This definition takes into consideration two aspect of social security—protective i.e., protection against falling living standards (prevention of vulnerability to deprivation) and promotional i.e., promoting living standards (prevention of deprivation).[2] Their definition implies that shortage of income is one of the most visible and crucial factors restricting the basic capabilities of many people to have access to various means of living. In addition to the problem of persistent deprivation, there is also, the issue of vulnerability be due to personal circumstances or on account of fluctuation in the social surroundings. Getubig also presents similar views:

> *"any kind of collective measures or activities designed to ensure that members of society meet their basic needs (such as adequate nutrition, shelter, health care and clean water supply), as well as being protected from contingencies (such as illness, disability, death, unemployment and old age) to enable them to maintain a standard of living consistent with social norms"* (quoted in Ginneken, 1997).

In developing countries like India, where majority of people is living in abject poverty and is engaged in agriculture and unorganised sector with low incomes, social security definition should encompass protective, preventive and promotional measures. It does not only comprise income security but also education, health, nutrition and employment securities and other welfare measures.

Existing Provisions

Social security to the workers is the responsibility of both the Centre and State Governments as it is enlisted in the concurrent list of the India Constitution. The various acts and schemes made so far in the country to protect the workers are actually applicable to about eight per cent labourforce engaged in organised sector. Although, Constitution of India has made provision to safeguard the interest of weaker sections, little has been done so far in this direction. Article 41 of the constitution under Directive Principles of State Policy says, *"The State shall, within the limits of its economic capacity and development, make effective provision for securing the right to work, to education and to public assistance in cases of unemployment, old age, sickness and disablement, and in other cases on under-served want."* Article 47 requires that the State should regard the raising of the level of nutrition and the standard of living of its people, and improvement of public health, as among its primary duties (Jhabvala and Sinha, 2001). However, even after 50 years of planned development, State could not provide effective social safety net to poor workers. During 1997, the United Front Government prepared a comprehensive Agricultural Workers Bill to guarantee minimum wages and better working conditions to agricultural workers. Sadly, several governments came in, but the bill could not be passed by the Parliament. It is understood that this central act could not be enacted due to opposition from states, as also from the bigger farmers to the payment of any cess for the constitution of a welfare fund for agricultural workers (Sankaran, 2001).

Social security measures adopted by the Government for unorganised sector workers may be divided into two categories. First category comprises all those measures, which are being adopted by the government to protect workers against falling living standards (protective measures) and the second category consists of those measures, which promote their living standards (promotional measures). Protective measures can further be divided into two groups: social insurance schemes and social assistance schemes. Social insurance schemes are financed mainly through contributions by employees and/or employers. Some social insurance schemes for the poor have also been financed by the government. Social assistance programmes provide some benefits to the target group of people and are financed from the general revenue of the state (Das, 1996). Both protective and promotional social security measures are quintessential for rural unorganised sector workers, as they are the most vulnerable section of the society.

A. Promotional Measures

The coverage under protective social security measures is inadequate. Therefore, emphasis is also being given to promotional measures of social security. They comprise two group i.e., self employment and wage-employment programmes. IRDP (1980), TRYSEM (1979) and DWCRA (1983) are the main self-employment programmes and JRY (1989) and EAS (1993) are the major wage-employment schemes. These programmes were launched by the government with the aim to provide income and employment securities to the rural poor labour.

1. Self-employment Programmes

TRYSEM was launched in 1979 as a centrally sponsored scheme to aim at providing basic technical skill and entrepreneurial skills to the rural youth in the age group of 18-35 years from the families below the poverty line. The programme enables them to take up self-employment in the broad fields of agriculture and allied sectors, industries, services and business activities. Under this scheme, a minimum of 50 per cent of youth should belong to SC/ST, 40 per cent should be women and three per cent of the trainees should be physically handicaped. The duration of training is normally 6 months and each trainee gets a stipend varying from Rs. 200 to Rs. 500 and a lump sum amount of Rs. 800 for purchasing toolkits. The share of the Centre and States is on 50:50 basis.

IRDP, which aims at providing income generating assets and self-employment opportunities for the rural poor, was launched in 1980. Assistance under this programme is given in the form of subsidy by the government and term credit by banks to below the poverty line (BPL) families. The beneficiary group consists of families of small and marginal farmers, agricultural labourers, rural artisan etc. District Rural Development Agency (DRDA) is the implementing agency for this programme. At the grassroots level, Block Development Office implements the programme with the assistance of the village level functionaries. In order to identify poor families, a BPL Census is conducted at the beginning of each plan period by the states. The Gram Sabha (GS) is involved in the identification and selection of beneficiaries under the programme from the initial stage itself.

It is noticed that in this programme forward and backward linkages were missing. There is also problem of the non-poor and not-so-poor gaining access to credit and subsidies under the programme at the expense of actual poor (Singh, 1998). Studies also observed that all IRDP beneficiary families could increase their income but only about 30 to 35 per cent of them crossed the poverty line (Ramachandraiah and Rao, 1998). Lack of group and cluster approach, deficiency of inputs, infrastructure and marketing support were other problems felt in the implementation of IRDP.

DWCRA, initially launched as a sub-scheme of IRDP during 1982-83 in 50 districts and subsequently extended to all districts in the country by 1994-95, aims at not only raising the income of rural women of poor households, but also enabling organised participation of group of women in the programmes of credit, skill training and infrastructure support for self-employment for rural women, who cannot take up economic activities individually on their own. The programme seeks to improve the access of rural women to health, education, safe drinking water, sanitation, nutrition, etc., thereby bringing about an improvement in the quality of the general welfare of women and children.

Our past experience shows that most of the self-employment schemes in rural area could not bear desired fruits because group entrepreneurship approach was not followed in these programmes. DWACRA was the only programme, which was based on this approach. However, due to lack of literacy and entrepreneurial skills among the rural women, the programme could not succeed in achieving the objectives for which it was made. Keeping in mind the limitation of earlier schemes, Government of India has launched a new self-employment scheme known as Swarnjayanti Gram Swarozgar Yojana (SGSY), which is based on group approach, on April 1, 1999. This scheme replaces the earlier self-employment and allied programmes—IRDP, TRYSEM, DWCRA, SITRA, GKY and MWS. It aims at establishing a large number of rural micro-enterprises. It is rooted in the belief that the rural poor in India have competencies and given the right support can be successful producers of valuable goods/services. This scheme is conceived as a holistic programme covering all aspects of self-employment, viz., organisation of the rural poor into self-help groups and their capacity building, planning of activity clusters, infrastructure build up, technology, credit and marketing. It is a credit-cum-subsidy programme. It envisages a greater involvement of the banks in the planning and preparation of projects, identification of activity clusters, infrastructure planning as well as capacity building and choice of activity of the SHGs. The programme also provides for promotion of marketing of the goods produced by the Swarozgaris. This would involve market intelligence, development of markets, consultancy services as well as institutional arrangements for marketing of the goods including exports. (For financial and physical progress of self-employment programmes, see Table-5.1)

TABLE 5.1
PHYSICAL AND FINANCIAL PROGRESS OF SELF-EMPLOYMENT PROGRAMMES

Year	*IRDP/SGSY*		*DWCRA*	
	Total Investment (Subsidy + Credit) (Rs. Crores)	*No. of families Assisted (Nos. in Lakh)*	*Central assistance Released (Rs. Lakh)*	*No. of Groups Formed*
1985-86	1171.15	30.60	630.70	6008
1986-87	1628.26	37.47	786.33	5545
1987-88	1902.79	42.47	607.29	4959
1988-89	2000.09	37.72	738.21	5968
1989-90	1985.96	33.51	901.00	5551
1990-91	1999.52	28.98	898.00	7139
1991-92	1163.19$	14.99$	962.72	9378
1992-93	1616.48	20.69	1548.17	9029
1993-94	2209.26	25.39	2365.00	15483
1994-95	2268.88	22.15	3100.00	37964
1995-96	2571.53	20.89	6365.00	37576
1996-97	2874.10	19.24	5696.00	41462
1997-98	2859.75	17.24	4145.43	36436
1998-99	1389.69#	7.82#		
1999-2000	2016.32	9.34 (292426)**	–	–
2000-2001	1057.84*	0.44* ((93017)**	–	–

Source: Compiled from various Annual Reports of Ministry of Rural Areas and Employment, Government of India, *$ till Dec. 1991, * till Dec. 2000, # till Nov. 1998, ** No. of SHGS.*

The emphasis of most of the programmes is only on the distribution aspect. But to solve the problem of unemployment and poverty, acceleration in the growth is as much necessary as its equitable distribution. Rural development implies both quantitative and qualitative change. Quantitatively, it is reflected in the increase in output, income and employment. Qualitatively, it refers to a better way of life, better health, education, housing and better environmental and institutional changes to ensure social justice. A high growth rate sustained over a long period is, therefore, a necessary condition for the country for achieving high level of employment and reducing poverty, but not a sufficient condition. Whether a high rate of economic growth would be able to generate sufficient employment in the economy actually depends on several factors such as nature of the growth, source of the growth, distribution of the growth, regional and sectoral pattern of the growth. Such growth helps poverty eradication that is sourced upon those sectors of the economy or those activities which have a natural tendency to involve the poor in their expansion (Hashim, 1998).

Therefore, to provide sustainable employment manifested in higher income to the workers of unorganised sector, growth oriented programmes should be dovetailed with poverty alleviation programmes. In this context, development of group entrepreneurship among the rural enterprising people can be the viable option. For this purpose, PRIs should identify the educated unemployed youths such those having diploma in engineering, ITIs and other management courses in their areas and organise them in a group for jointly taking up some enterprising projects. Banks should also help in advancing loans to such group. Such group can be integrated with SGSY. Agro and non-agro based rural small-scale industries may be established in joint venture involving educated skilled unemployed youth of the area, unskilled rural poor people and gram panchayats at the block level. These industries should be based on the locally available resources and skill. The funds of such industries may be mobilised through bank loans and subsidy given to the target groups. The beneficiaries should be given a formal training for two to three months and then be absorbed in these industries. Thus, the employees will be able to generate sustained income for their families. Over and above their salaries, they will get dividends for their share capital (Singh and Ali, 1997). Panchayat Udyogs (PUs)—rural micro enterprises initiated at the behest of gram panchayats to provide employment to rural artisans and other weaker sections, and to ensure proper utilisation of local available resources, can also be involved in group entrepreneurship drive.

2. Wage-employment Programmes

The main objectives of wage-employment programmes are to create gainful employment to rural poor and to develop socio-economic infrastructure in the rural areas. The earliest programme for providing wage employment was the *Food for Work* programme launched in 1970. Subsequently, other programmes like National Rural Employment Programme (NREP) and Rural Landless Employment Guarantee Programme (RLEGP) were implemented. Later on, they were merged together and a new scheme—Jawahar Rozgar Yojana (JRY) was implemented from 1 April 1989. Two another schemes—Employment Assurance Scheme (1993) and MP Local Area Development Scheme (1993) were also introduced subsequently with the same purpose.

A distinctive feature of JRY is that it is implemented by gram panchayats. DRDAs/Zilla parishads receive funds from the Union/State Governments and release them to different gram panchayats based on criteria set out in JRY guidelines. Gram panchayats prepare a shelf of projects at panchayat circle/village-level and undertake the works after technical approval of panchayat samities and release of funds based on the District Annual Action Plan. The overall planning, coordination, supervision, reviews and monitoring of the programme is the responsibility of the implementing agencies at the district level The Centre and States share the programme outlay in the ratio of 80:20.

Initially launched in 1778 development blocks of 261 districts situated in the drought prone, desert, tribal and hill areas, Employment Assuranace Scheme (EAS) is being implemented in all the development blocks of the country since 1997-98. The primary objective of the scheme is to create additional wage employment opportunities through manual work for the rural poor living below the poverty line during lean agricultural season and the secondary objective is the creation of durable socio-economic community assets for sustained employment and development. The scheme is being implemented as a centrally sponsored scheme on cost sharing basis between the centre and the states in the ratio of 80:20.

In order to the create demand driven village infrastructure including durable assets and generate supplementary employment for the unemployed poor in the rural areas, Jawahar Gram Samridhi Yojana (JGSY) was launched on April 1, 1999 as a modified version of JRY. The scheme is being implemented by gram panchayats (GPs). District Rural Development Agencies (DRDAs)/Zilla Parishads (ZPs) release the funds including state matching share directly to GPs. Twenty-two and a half per cent of JGSY funds have been earmarked for individual beneficiary schemes for SCs/STs. Three per cent annual allocation would be utilised for creation of barrier free infrastructure for the disabled. DRDA/ZP and KP will be responsible for overall guidance, coordination, supervision, monitoring and periodical reporting. (For physical and financial progress of JRY/JGSY and EAS, see Table 5.2)

TABLE 5.2
PHYSICAL AND FINANCIAL PROGRESS OF WAGE-EMPLOYMENT PROGRAMMES

Year	*JRY/JGSY*		*EAS*	
	Expenditure in Rs. crores	*Mandays generated in Lakh*	*Expenditure in Rs. crores*	*Mandays generated in Lakh*
1989-90 to 1991-92	7709.33	25481.47	–	–
1992-93	2709.59	7821.02	–	–
1993-94	3878.71	10258.40	183.75	44.74
1994-95	4268.33	9517.07	1235.45	2739.56
1995-96	4466.91	8958.25	1720.61	3465.27
1996-97	2163.98	4006.32	2160.41	4030.02
1997-98	2451.65	3960.79	2307.95	3816.77
1998-99	1243.71*	1902.80*	2882.18	4279.36
1999-2000	2035.27	2683.03	2182.60	2786.17
2000-2001	711.35**	885.12**	650.16**	745.24**

Source: Compiled from various Annual Reports of Ministry of Rural Areas and Employment, Government of India. *up to Nov. 1998, **up to December 2000.

Studies conducted by researchers and the concurrent evaluations identify several weaknesses of JRY. For instance, studies in U.P. and Andhra Pradesh reveal that JRY is able to provide only 15-20 days employment for about five to seven families (Rajakutty, 1998).[3] Guhan (1995) finds that transfers via wage payments per se are a very expensive and inefficient approach to help the poor. Of the one rupee spent on JRY only 14 paise are likely to reach the poor via effective net wage transfer.

B. Protective Measures

Protective social security provisions for unorganised sector workers are as follows:

- Landless Agricultural Labour Group Insurance Scheme under which all landless agricultural labourers have been covered for a uniform sum assured of Rs. 2000. The entire premium is met from Social Security Fund.
- The National Social Assistance Programme (NSAP), which comprises three Schemes, namely, National Old Age Pension Scheme (NOAPS), National Family Benefit Scheme (NFBS) and National Maternity Benefit Scheme (NMBS), was launched by GOI in 1995-96 as a centrally sponsored programme. Under NOAPS, each poor person beyond the age of 65 gets Rs. 75 per month as pension. Under NFBS, lump sum survivor benefit of Rs. 5000 in case of natural death and Rs. 10000 in case of accidental death of the main bread earner is given to the family of the deceased. Under NMBS, lumpsum cash assistance of Rs. 500 is given to the pregnant woman of the household living below the poverty line up to the first two live births provided she is 19 years of age or above. NSAP is implemented by the district level implementing authorities headed by the District Collector/ Magistrate/Deputy Commissioner. To make the scheme more responsive and cost effective, cooperation of the panchayats and municipalities is sought in the delivery of social assistance. The

financial and physical progress under the NOAPS has been relatively better as compared to the other two schemes. Out of total Rs. 546.28 crores spent on these schemes during 2000-01 (till December 2000), Rs. 347.62 crores were spent on NOAPS covering 55.45 lakh beneficiaries. The coverage under the other two schemes was rather limited, one lakh under the NFBS and 6.46 lakh under the NMBS with an expenditure of Rs. 142.86 crore and Rs. 55.28 crores respectively.

- Rural Group Insurance Scheme under which all people in the age group 20-25 years will be given life insurance cover of Rs. 5000 at the annual premium of Rs. 60 for those below 40 and Rs. 70 for those above 40 years of age. Central and state governments bear jointly half of the premium for the poor. The scheme is being implemented by LIC with the involvement of intermediate level panchayat.
- Food for Education Programme under which family of a child labourer will be given one kg cereal per day if the child is taken off from the hazardous job and sent to school.
- Annapurna Scheme, under which an elderly destitute is provided with 10 kilograms of wheat or rice free of cost through the existing public distribution. The scheme will be quite effective in improving the food security of the poor elder people. This scheme is beneficial particularly for elderly women, as, besides poverty, the incidence of widowhood is a major factor explaining the vulnerability of the elderly women. According to 1991 census, half of the elderly women in India were either widowed, divorced or separated (Rajan, 2001). As the life expectancy of female in particular, and, all population in general, has been increasing census after census, social security scheme like Annapurna would be quite effective to take care of nutritional problem of elderly rural destitute. During 2000-01, an amount of Rs. 100 crores have been provided for the scheme. This would enable to

cover 13.47 lakh elderly poor people.

- Ministry of Social Justice and Empowerment commissioned a national project title "OASIS" (Old Age Social and Income Security) and nominated an eight member Expert Committee to examine the policy questions concerned with old age income security in India. The research and recommendation under the project focus on improving existing provisions, and to devise a new pension provision for the excluded workers who are capable of saving, albeit, modest amounts, and converting this saving into an old age income security provision. The rise in old-age dependency ratio has long term implications for pension schemes. As the life expectancy rises, people will have the capacity to remain active in the labour force longer. To ensure the contribution of the older people to the society, employment opportunities will have to be created for them so that they may contribute to pension funds on their own.
- Beneficiaries of IRDP have also been provided insurance cover. Under IRDP, a sum of Rs. 5000 is paid on the death of beneficiary to his family if death occurs within 5 years after taking loan from the bank. In case of accidental death, the amount to be paid to the family of the deceased is Rs. 10000. About 2.12 crores IRDP beneficiaries have provided insurance cover.
- Recently Government of India with the collaboration of LIC of India launched an ambitious *Krishi Shramik Samajik Suraksha Yojana* 2001 for agricultural labourers. The scheme is initially introduced in 50 blocks but will gradually be extended to all blocks of the country. The scheme will provide life insurance, pensions, and disability benefits to the agricultural labourers.

Besides these schemes, a few states have also made welfare schemes for rural labour such as Group Insurance Scheme for Landless Agricultural Labourers of the State of

Gujarat; Scheme for Financial Assistance to Landless Women Agricultural labourers during pregnancy of the State of Gujarat; Kerala Agricultural Workers' Pension Scheme; Andhra Pradesh Landless Agricultural workers' Pension Scheme, Old Age Pension (Destitute Agricultural Labourers) Scheme of Tamil Nadu, Asha Kiran Scheme of the Government of Karnataka etc. Child Labour (Prohibition and Regulation) Act, 1986, gives protection to the agricultural workers (Srinivasan, 1999).

Thus, southern states have more social security provisions for unorganised workers than their counterparts in other regions of the country. Kerala is the foremost state among them in introducing various welfare schemes for the poor. This state has initiated some measures to provide social security to workers in the wide range of activities in the unorganised sector. In spite of relatively having low economic growth, Kerala has the highest human development level. Direct action on health and education are responsible for its success in improved levels of living. People's participation and involvement in various rural development programmes through Panchayat Raj Institutions in the state have enhanced the efficiency of delivery of various rural development programmes. The extent of people participation (both physically and financially) in the state can be seen from the 9th plan estimate of one GP (Kadakkavoor GP under Chirayinkeezhu block of Thiruvananthapuram). The 9th plan estimate of this GP is Rs. 5.07 crores, comprising Rs. 2.12 from grant-in-aid from the state government, Rs. 0.67 crore loan from financial institutions and Rs. 2.19 crores from contribution from community/beneficiaries in labour, material and money (Bandyopadhyay, 1997). Thus, for each rupee of state grant-in-aid, GP is putting in more than one rupee; while in other state like U.P., no such effort has yet been made.

The above discussion reveals that social security has regional dimension. Some states are doing well in the area of social security, while others do not have adequate provision yet for protecting the poor against personal and covariate risks. The success of grassroots planning and governance in Kerala evinces that resource constraints can not come in the way of managmg rural development, if effective people's participation is ensured in the conception, planning and implementation of various socio-economic schemes based on felt-need of the people and locally available physical and human resources; public service delivery mechanism is improved through better physical infrastructure and motivated staff. The discussion also reveals that the unorganised sector workers mostly depend on the redistributive and poverty-alleviation types of social safety nets. In fact, the combined coverage under protective and promotional measures is very limited. Moreover, funds under different social security schemes are routed through different channels without any proper coordination and cohesion due to lack of evolvement of effective delivery mechanism.

Institutional Arrangement

Unorganised rural labourers are the most neglected and deprived section of the rural society. To improve their situation in terms of better access to health, education, food and shelter and to protect them from personal and covariate risks, there is need to develop an efficient institutional arrangement for designing, implementing and monitoring social security schemes. Jutting (1999) identifies four broad categories of social security systems prevailing in developing countries: State-based systems, market-based systems, member organisations-based systems, and private household-based systems.

In India, the state and state-initiated organisations have been implementing various social security schemes, but there is not wide coverage of workers under these schemes. Except execution of some employment and poverty alleviation programmes and few social assistance schemes, unorganised sector workers do not have any comprehensive social security provision. The expenditure on social security schemes is not adequate. It is obvious from the fact that during early 1990s, total expenditure on both promotional and protective social security programmes at the level of 15 major Indian states constituted only 2.63 per cent of state domestic product (SDP) and 16.63 per cent of total revenue expenditure (Prabhu and Sandhya, 2001). However, the expenditure on protective schemes comprised merely 0.26 per cent of SDP and 1.67 per cent of total revenue expenditure. Although, few more protective social security schemes were launched by the Government during the late 1990s, the expenditure incurred on all these schemes was insignificant in relation to the magnitude of deprivation in the country. In addition to the meagre funds allocated to these schemes, another problem with them is that they are not being implemented efficiently.[4]

State should play a major role in providing social security to rural workers. However, mobilisation of adequate funds to finance the social security programmes has become the major constraint on the part of the government because of increasing fiscal deficit and increase in non-plan expenditure (interest payment on central government debt, defence expenditure, subsidy and administrative expenses). The structural adjustment programmes (macro economic contraction) and process of liberalisation and globalisation initiated during 1991 and thereafter have actually undermined the role of government on the one hand and have increased job insecurity among workers on the other. Existing funds for social security are grossly inadequate and need to be augmented. There may be various options to raise the funds for social security. The Human Development Report (1990) suggests the following for financing social security:

"(a) Taxes: Raising of extra resources by reducing tax avoidance and tax evasion; (b) Discriminating user fees: Improvement in social services so that better off pay for services, poor sections pay nothing more than nominal fees, particularly for primary education and primary health care; (c) Voluntary organisation contributions; (d) reallocating

budgetary resources within sectors: Shifting expenditure from low priority to high priority uses-say from curative to preventive health or from tertiary to primary education; (e) reordering budgetary priority across sectors: Shifting expenditure on military to social sector."

Another promising area for raising resources for financing social security is the agricultural sector. At present, agricultural income is out of purview of income tax. There are one crore agricultural holdings (i.e., 10 per cent of total operational holdings) over 4 hectares, which comprise 49 per cent of total cultivated area. If government imposes a nominal tax on the income of these farmers, crores of rupees can be mobilised for this purpose. The income assessment can easily be done by the revenue staff (patwari etc.) of state government without any extra expenditure. The only need is to generate political consensus and will power on this issue. Income for social security can also be mobilised through donations. If 100 per cent rebate is given for income tax benefits to those who donate money for social security fund, people may come forward to donate money for this purpose.

However, availability of funds for social security is necessary, but not the sufficient condition; the determining factors are the appropriate policy framework, formulation of suitable schemes with the involvement of beneficiaries and effective delivery system. Presently, a number of centrally sponsored schemes (promotional as well as protective) are being implemented by GOI in rural areas, they are being implemented by different departments/agencies and due to lack of coordination among various departments, schemes with similar objectives are targeting the same population.[5] The Approach Paper to Tenth Five-Year Plan makes a candid remark:

"Most schemes follow a blueprint and top-down approach, with little flexibility given to field staff. Any change in the scheme requires approval from GOI which is time consuming. Uniformity of schemes all over the country from Mizoram to

> *Kerala, without sufficient delegation to states to change the schemes to suit local conditions, leads to a situation where the states even knowing that the scheme is not doing well become indifferent to its implementation"* (GOI, 2001).

It also identifies several deficiencies in the implementation of centrally sponsored schemes (CSSs) such as: emphasis on expenditure rather than on attainment of objectives, releasing of funds in the end of financial year, too many schemes to be effectively implemented, and unwillingness to accept poor performance for the fear of being questioned in parliament or adverse press publicity etc. To overcome these deficiencies, there is a need to develop an alternative institutional framework for implementation and monitoring of CSSs. Presently, these schemes are being implemented through DRDA.

Under 73rd Constitutional Amendment Act, Panchayat Raj Institutions (PRIs) have been assigned the responsibility of preparation and implementation of plans of economic development and social justice in rural areas. Under this new dispensation, almost all the promotional and protective social security schemes have constitutionally come under the purview of PRIs, but due to repugnance of government officials and unfriendly attitude of state and central level political leaders, PRIs still could not be entrusted with all the 29 items of works as enlisted in the 11th schedule of the Constitution in most of the states. There is, therefore, need to transfer all these social security schemes to three-tier system of panchayt in real term, not merely on paper.

Due to representation of women and other weaker sections of society in panchayat, a new dynamic social change is taking place. The weaker and the poorer sections will now have greater stake in panchayats. Despite certain limitations, reservation of SC/ST, women and other weaker sections in panchayats will help in developing the required leadership to move up the ladder in governing their own affairs in the rural areas. In a way, the mandatory elections of SC/ST and female candidates are likely to change the socio-economic dynamics in the rural areas. These groups have now occupied formal positions in a fairly large number across the states, leading to a silent socio-political revolution in the rural power structure. Their participation is expected to enable the local bodies to be more sensitive to the needs and aspirations of the poor people. However, questions are often raised about the capability of PRIs in managing rural development schemes. It is true that even after 8 years of implementation of new Panchayat Raj System in the country, PRIs do not have adequate power, finance, and planning infrastructure at all the three levels. Instead of building the capacity of PRIs, Government of India is running a parallel institution (DRDA) at the district level to implement various CSSs. There is urgency now to dismantle DRDA and to hand over all the CSSs to PRIs. It is necessary that the funds earmarked for social security should directly be transferred to PRIs at different levels on the recommendation of central and state finance commissions and panchayats should be given full autonomy in planning and implementation of programmes based on the felt-need of different areas. For effective planning and execution of these schemes, stress must be on the capacity building of PRIs. For this, top priority must be given to develop the human resources for panchayt. At present, the staff of panchayat in several states in neither adequate nor competent to perform the various managerial functions of the organisation. Therefore, besides imparting training to the exiting staff and elected representatives, future recruitment should be made from the candidates having degree/diploma in rural management (Singh, 2001).

In addition to strengthening the PRI at district, block and village levels as an alternative institutional arrangement for planning, execution and monitoring of social security schemes, member-based organisations system should also be promoted through the involvement of Voluntary Organisation because they were found quite effective in protecting their members against personal as well as covariate risks. In this context, two successful examples can be cited. One is the Grameen Bank of Bangladesh and other is Self-Employed Women Association (SEWA) in the state of Gujarat (India).

Established in 1983 by Prof. Yunus of Chittagong University with the help of rural poor women, the Grameen Bank today serves two million borrowers and works in 34000 villages, having 1041 branches and 11000 staff members. Group-based lending, taking the bank to the poor rather than having poor come to the bank, a focus on women and a system of regular weekly installments for repayment of loans are the four pillars in the success of the bank. Apart from providing credit facilities to its members, the bank is also providing health and education securities to the families of its members. Grameen Bank also organises workshops to train its members in various areas including health and nutrition and other social issues. It has also extended loans to the members for constructing houses in rural areas (Yunus, 1997).

SEWA is a union of 2.2 lakh women workers of the unorganised sector established by Ela R. Bhatt in 1972. SEWA bank, which was initially made with the contribution of a day's earnings of 4000 women, has now 125000 depositors and a working capital of over Rs. 300 million. SEWA provides health care, child-care, insurance and shelter services to its members. It carries out health services in a decentralised way by district level health teams. With intensive training and support, its team of 200 midwives and health workers serve as health educators-cum-barefoot doctors for women workers. It also coordinates with local government in programmes to upgrade slums, bringing water, sanitation, toilets, and basic amenities to the rural and urban poorest communities (Chatterjee, *www.sewa.org*).

There is a need to encourage member-based organisations systems of social security. In this regard, the role of voluntary organisations operating in rural areas may be very vital in organising the unorganised labourers in self-help groups. Since, the number of attached labourers has been continuously declining and the number of casual and contact labourers in agriculture has been on rise, formation of such groups will be feasible as well as desirable.

Market-based systems have little significance in context of providing social security to poor labourers. Market is guided by the profit, which depends on demand and cost of the social security services. The demand for social security in the market will depend on the income level of workers and the degree of risks associated with the job of workers. According to Jutting (1999):

> *"In most developing countries commercial insurance contracts are available but the access to them is mainly limited to the wealthier section of the population and to people living in urban centre. A high risk environment, combined with lack of resources, a weak infrastructure and information problems between the insurer and the insured lead to high unit transaction costs per insurance contact and therefore high premiums, which cannot be paid by the majority of the population."*

Concluding Remarks

This paper examines the existing social security measures for rural labour and suggests an institutional framework for efficient and cost-effective delivery of various promotional and protective social security programmes. As social security is enlisted in the concurrent list of the Indian Constitution, it is the responsibility of both the Centre and the state governments. Although, they have been implementing various social security schemes, there has not been a wide coverage of workers under these schemes. Except some rural development programmes and a few social assistance schemes, unorganised sector workers do not have any comprehensive social security provision. Hence, to improve their situation in terms of better access to health, education, food, and shelter and to protect them from personal and covariate risks, there is a need to develop an efficient institutional arrangement for designing, implementing and monitoring of the social security schemes.

After 73rd Constitutional Amendment Act, almost all the promotional and protective social security schemes have come under the purview of PRIs. However, due to repugnance of government officials and unfriendly attitude of state and central level political leaders, they could not become the real institutions of decentralised planning and governance. Instead of building the capacity of PRIs, Government of India is running a parallel institution (DRDA) at the district level to implement various CSSs. There is now need to dismantle DRDA and to empower PRI as an institution for implementation of various rural development schemes including social security at district, block and village levels. Since different regions have different problems, any scheme uniformly implemented in all areas may not prove effective. It is necessary that the funds earmarked for social security should directly be transferred to PRIs at different levels on the recommendation of central and state finance commissions and panchayats should be given full autonomy in planning and implementation of programmes based on the felt-need of different areas. To make PRIs effective in delivering services emphasis must be laid on the capacity building; for this purpose top priority must be accorded to the development of the human resource, physical and planning infrastructure, and sound information system for panchayats. In addition to strengthening the PRI, member-based organisations system should also be promoted through the involvement of voluntary organisations.

REFERENCES

1. The vulnerability to deprivation has regional dimensions. Rural workers of distress regions, which are prone to chronic drought and famine, are most deprived. For instance, the helpless tribals of Kashipur (Orissa) consumed mango kernels and wild roots to survive, as they did not have money to buy even the cheap PDS rice. Empirical study made by Rajuladevi (2001) on agricultural labour households reveals that the majority of agricultural labourers in distress regions survived on cereals and had only one

meal per day, particularly during the slack season—a stark indicator of food insecurity. Her study also describes how the agricultural labourers went hand in hand with other forms of deprivation.

2. For other similar definitions of social security for developing countries see: Guhan (1994) Mahendra Dev (1996), Ginneken (1997), and Rodgers (1999).
3. If opportunity cost of employment in JRY is taken into consideration, the actual employment received by the beneficiaries may be somewhat lower than what is recorded in the register. For instance, a study made by Mahi Pal (1999) finds that the net employment benefits an average worker in Rampur Maniharan block of Saharanpur district of U.P. got was 9.67 persondays as against 12.02 persondays he actually received in JRY in 1992-93.
4. Evaluation studies made by several scholars as well as concurrent evaluation made by Ministry of Rural Development, Government of India, reveal this fact. For example, Rajan (2001) finds several problems in the implementation of Old Age Pension Scheme such as problem in identification of genuine beneficiaries. Approach Paper to Tenth Plan also highlights the deficiencies in the implementation of various CSSs.
5. Guhan (1995) reveals that the Centre, in order to demonstrate that the New Economic Policy has a human face, has quantitatively expanded the rural development schemes with progressively higher financial allocation without any attempt to reform or restructure them in the light of the shortcomings evident from numerous evaluations.

Bandyopadhyay, D. (1997), "People's Participation in Planning; Kerala Experiment", *Economic & Political Weekly,* Vol. XXXII (39), September 27-October 3, pp. 2450-2454.

Chatterjee, M.(-), "My Health: My Asset and My Right—A Case Study of the Self-Employment Women's Association in Gujarat, India", *http://www.sewa.org*.

Das, S.K. (1996), Social Security for the Unorganised Poor", *Journal of Rural Development,* Vol. 15(3), September-October, pp. 339-335.

Dev, S. Mahendra (2001), "Social Security: Performance, Issues and Policies" in S. Mahendra Dev at el. (ed.) *Social and Economic Security in India,* Institute of Human Development, New Delhi, pp. 27-59.

Drèze, J and Sen, A. 1991. "Public Action for Social Security: Foundations and Strategy", in E. Ahead, J. Drèze, J. Hills and A. Sen (eds.): *Social Security in Developing Countries* (Oxford, Clarendon Press), pp. 1-40.

Government of India (2001), "Approach Paper to Tenth Plan (2002-

2007), *Planning Commission,* New Delhi, pp. 48-51.

Guhan, S. 1994, "Social Security Options for Developing Countries", International *Labour Review* Geneva, 133(1) pp. 35-53.

Hashim, H.R. (1998), "Poverty Alleviation Programmes in India: An Overview" in R.C. Choudhry and S. Rajakutty (ed.) *Fifty Years of Rural Development in India: Retrospect and Prospect,* Vol. I, NIRD, Hyderabad, pp. XXVI-XLI.

Jhabvala, R. and Singh, S. (2001), "Social Security for Women Workers in the Unorganised Sector" *The Indian Journal of Labour Economics,* Vol. 44(4), October-December pp. 577-584.

Jutting, J. (1999), "Social Security Systems in Low Income Countries: An Overview from an Institutional Perspective", *The Indian Journal of Labour Economics,* Vol. 42(3), July-September, pp 341-360.

ILO (1984), "Introduction to Social Security", *International Labour Organisation,* Geneva, p. 3.

Pal, Mahi (1999), *Capital Formation and Employment Generation in Rural India,* Mittal Publications, New Delhi.

Prabhu, K. Sita and Sandhya V. Iyer (2001), "Financing Social Security: A Human Development Perspective" in S. Mahendra Dev at el. (ed.) *Social and Economic Security in India,* Institute of Human Development, New Delhi, pp. 83-99.

Rajakutty, S. (1998), "Wage Employment Programmes: A Review" in R.C. Choudhry and S. Rajakutty (ed.), Vol. I, pp. 245-259.

Rajan, S Irudaya (2001), "Social Assistance for Poor Elderly: How Effective?" *The Economic and Political Weekly,* Feb. 24, pp. 613-617.

Rajuladevi, A.K. (2001), "Food Poverty and Consumption among Landless Labour Households", *Economic and Political Weekly,* July 14, pp. 2656-2664.

Rodgers G. (1999), "Poverty, Exclusion and Insecurity: Issues and Policy Frameworks", *The Indian Journal of Labour Economics,* Vol. 42(3), July-September, pp. 327-340.

Sankaran, T.S. (2001), "Social Security for Workers in Unorganised Sector", in A. Kundu and A.N. Sharma (ed.) *Informal Sector in India,* Institute of Human Development, New Delhi, pp. 405-412.

Singh R.P. (1998), "Poverty alleviation Strategies in India: An Overview", in R.C. Choudhry and S. Rajakutty (ed.) Vol. I, pp. 1-30.

Singh, S.P. and M. Ali (1996-97), "Unorganised Sector Workers and Social Security: Some Challenges and Tasks Ahead", Varta, Vol. XVII & XVIII, Nos. 1 & 2, April-October, pp. 61-73.

Singh, S.P. (2001), "Management of People by Gram Panchayat for Rural Development", Journal of Rural Development, Vol 20(2), April-June, pp. 219-252.

Srinivasan, M.V. (1999), "Neglect of the Agricultural workforce", *www.index-labour-99.htm.*

Van Ginneken, W. (1997), "Social Security for the Informal Sector: Issues, Options and Tasks Ahead", Working Paper, ILO, Geneva, *http://www.ilo.org*.

Yunus, M. (1998), "The Grameen Bank Story: Rural Credit in Bangladesh", in A. Krishna, N. Uphoff and M.J. Esman (ed.) *Reason for Hope: Instructive Experiences in Rural Development*, Vistaar Publications, New Delhi, pp. 9-24.

6

SOCIAL SECURITY FOR RURAL LABOUR IN INDIA

Vipla Chopra

Introduction

Social Security is considered in all the countries of the world as *sine qua non* of the economic system an important tool for removing unemployment, poverty and sickness. It is one of the dynamic concepts of the modern age, which is influencing social and economic policies of every nation of the world. Considering the importance of Social Security, the International Social Security Association rightly said, "no peace without social justice and no justice without Social Security." Social Security has been on top of the priority agenda of the International Labour Organization (ILO). Of the world's more than 2000 million labour force, only 40 per cent are socially protected and the rest 60 per cent are unprotected. Of these 77 per cent are living in the developing countries, including India.

Germany was among the pioneers who took up the problem of social security more seriously. Social security originated in Germany in 1881. Austria, Hungary, Norway and most of the European countries also introduced social security programmes in the late 19th century. In U.S.A, the social security Act, 1935 provided all social security benefits. Similarly in New Zeland and Great Britain different schemes of social security were introduced suitable to their countries requirements. The measures of social security varied from country to country. The widespread progress of social security schemes in different countries has been largely due to the efforts and activities of the ILO.

Broadly speaking, the term "Social Security" is usually employed to indicate "specific government programmes designed primarly to prevent want by assuring to families the basic means of subsistence." Friedlander defines social security as, "programme of protection provided by society against these contingencies of modern life..... sickness, unemployment, old age, dependency, industrial accidents and invalidism against which the individual cannot be expected to protect him and his family by his own ability or foresight." Taken in its widest sense, social security means the 'security of the whole society.' This concept is so wide that it encompasses all activities of mankind. However, the term as commonly used connotes measures for economic security only under government auspices and such economic security in developing countries like India does not extend to all members of the the society, but only to some restricted classes of people like industrial labour, government employees etc. A coverage of the programmes under social security would be clear from the following definition put forward by Lord William Beveridge, "The term 'social security' is used to denote the security of an income to take the place of earnings when they are interrupted by unemployment, sickness or accident, to provide for retirement through age, to provide for loss of support by the death of another person, and to meet an exceptional expenditure, such as those connected with birth, death and marriage."

Although social security measures had been introduced in many countries decades ago, in India, they were introduced only after 1947. There has been very little discussion on social security in Indian Plan documents. In India social security measures are usually divided into two categories:

(i) Protective measures such as medical care and benefits relating to old age, maternity, sickness, survival, etc.

(ii) Promotional measures such as wage employment, self-employment, health and education, etc.

In India some restricted classes of people like industrial labour, government employees etc. enjoy social security. In India out of 397 million workers in 1999-2000 only 28.11 million (i.e., about 7 per cent of total employment) in the organized sector were covered by protective social security measures and the rest 268.89 million (i.e. 93 per cent) belonging to unorganized sector were covered by promotional security measures. Thus a large chunk of labour, especially in the agricultural sector and in organized sector is outside the purview of the social security legislation. The constitution of India in its Directive Principles of State Policy laid down that the state should make "effective provision for securing the right to public assistance in case of unemployment, old age, sickness and disablement and in other cases of undeserved want." Realising the importance of social security as an essential component of labour policy in India, the government took several measures. A beginning in social security in India was made in 1923 when Workmen's Compensation Act was passed. The Act is very wide in coverage and covers many diverse industries. The Act was suitably revised. Maternity Benefit Act, 1961, which regulates the employment of women in certain establishment, was another important step taken by the government. Another most important step in the field of social security was taken in 1948 when the Employees' State Insurance (ESI) Act, 1948 was passed. The ESI Act provides medical benefit, sickness benefit, disablement benefit, maternity benefit, dependents' benefit and the funeral benefit. Later Provident fund and gratuity schemes were also introduced. But these benefits were enjoyed by the organized sector.

Recently, GOI has proposed to extend some of the benefits widely enjoyed in the organized sector to the poorest of the poor in the unorganized sector-these are pensions, survivor benefits (the equivalent of family pension on the death of retired employees) and maternity benefits.

Several State governments have also attempted to provide various protective social security measures for the unorganized poor and vulnerable sections of the society. In the 2001-2002 budget, the Insurance Regulatory and Development Authority (IRDA) was instituted to chart out a road map for a new pension scheme so that the unorganized sector is provided with adequate social security cover. Even in the insurance sector the government has introduced Khetihar Mazdoor Bima Yojana aimed at retrenched workers. The Finance Minister in the budget 2002-03 has also proposed the setting up of a new Corporation for Agriculture Insurance to be promoted by the existing public sector general insurance companies. This move if implemented, will go a long way in boosting the present infrastructure for agricultural insurance, which is currently very weak in our country. Close monitoring of pension scheme for the unorganized sector is one of the major requirement. Even in the 1995-96 budget, government for the first time made an attempt to introduce protective measures of social security at the national level. The Finance Minister introduced in the budget a National Social Assistance Scheme to help the unorganized and vulnerable sections.

To increase the well being of the poor and vulnerable sections in particular, various components of social security like employment, education, shelter, health and other basic needs become significant. Amongst the most deprived and disadvantaged group in India, rural labour is one of them. They are mostly employed in the unorganized sector in agricultural or non-agricultural activities, which clearly warrants the tremendous importance of social security for them.

In India agriculture is the basic industry and provides employment to 65 per cent of India's labour force. According to 1991 census, the agricultural workers constituted 58.99 per cent of the total work force, and of total agricultural workers 40.26 per cent were agricultural labourers. The growth rate in the number of agricultural labourers during 1981-91 was 34.41 per cent. These agricultural workers are in dire need of social security. They don't enjoy sickness leave, medical benefits, old age benefits etc. Even female agricultural labourers (which constituted 38.12 per cent of the total agricultural labourers in 1991) don't enjoy any maternity benefits. Besides these workers who are engaged in agricultural activities, there are number of people who work as rural artisans, rickshaw pullers, cobblers etc. who have no social security. Women, children, elderly people working in rural areas are also deprived of social security benefits. Due to modernization and economic pressure, joint family system is becoming unpopular even in rural sector. A new social order is gradually and silently replacing the old joint family system. Therefore a firm policy on social security for rural population is immensely needed.

The present paper addresses to three major issues:

One, various forms of social insecurities facing rural labour;

Two, recent measures introduced by Govt. of India to improve the lot of rural poor,

Three, to suggest ways to improve social security for rural labour.

The study has been confined to India as a whole.

Types of Social Securities

Rural labour in India suffers from various forms of social insecurities like income, employment, land, food and nutrition, education, health etc.

Income Security

In a country as large as India poverty is endemic in vast tracts of the countryside, and is concentrated largely among rural labour. Among the rural labourers, agricultural labourers suffer from severe income insecurity because they are landless and earn low wages. After independence Government of India introduced various land reforms like abolition of Zamindari system, Tenancy reforms, Ceilings on land holdings, Consolidation of holdings etc. to protect the interests of landless labourers, small and marginal farmers. But these land reform laws were not effectively implemented because of lack of political will on the part of authorities. As a result of these reforms, poverty ratio has declined in rural India, though rural poverty ratio remained higher than urban poverty ratio throughout the period 1973-74 to 1999-2000 (Table 6.1). In absolute terms, the number of poor in rural areas has been more than the number of poor in urban areas throughout the period 1973-74 to 1999-2000.

TABLE 6.1
ESTIMATES OF POVERTY

Year	*All India Number (Million)*	*Poverty Ratio (per cent)*	*Rural Number (Million)*	*Poverty Ratio (per cent)*	*Urban Number (Million)*	*Poverty Ratio (per cent)*
1973-74	321	54.9	261	56.4	60	49.0
1977-78	329	51.3	264	53.1	65	45.2
1983	323	44.5	252	45.7	71	40.8
1987-88	307	38.9	232	39.1	75	38.2
1993-94	320	36.0	244	37.3	76	32.4
1999-2000	260	26.1	193	27.1	67	23.6

Source: Planning commission.

Agricultural labour, construction workers and many other wage workers in the rural segment are covered by Minimum Wages Act 1948. Minimum Wages are in operation in almost all the states. Although different state governments have revised the minimum wages, the wages fixed are still very low for the unorganized workers.

Employment Security

Not only the magnitude of rural unemployment has been increasing but uncertainty of employment is also on the rise. Estimates of unemployment prepared by Planning Commission as on April 1, 1990 by Usual Principal Status (UPS), Current Weekly Status (CWS) and by Current Daily Status have been presented in Table 6.2. In each case rural unemployment is more than the urban unemployment.

N.S.S. Organisation has made another estimate of rural unemployment over a period of time (Table 6.3) It is clear from this Table that the magnitude of rural unemployment

TABLE 6.2
ESTIMATES OF UNEMPLOYMENT

Million

	Male	*Female*	*Total*
1. By Usual Principal Status (UPS)			
Rural	4.97	2.66	7.63
Urban	4.16	1.30	5.46
Total	9.13	3.96	13.05
2. By Current Weekly Status (CWS)			
Rural	7.06	2.92	9.98
Urban	4.59	1.31	5.90
Total	11.65	4.23	15.88
3. By Current Daily Status (CDS)			
Rural	7.75	4.59	12.34
Urban	5.91	1.66	7.57
Total	13.66	6.25	19.90

Note: These figures related to the population in age group 5+.
Source: Planning Commission, Employment: past trends and Prospects for 1990s (May 1990), p. 15.

TABLE 6.3
RURAL UNEMPLOYMENT IN INDIA
(% OF RURAL LABOUR FORCE)

	Male			*Female*		
Round and the period covered	*Urban Status*	*Status*	*Daily Status*	*Urban Status*	*Status*	*Daily Status*
27th, Oct. 1972-Sep. 1973	0.75	2.22	4.75	0.18	2.26	3.70
32nd, July 1977-June 1978	1.41	2.34	4.45	1.68	1.40	2.45
38th, Jan. 1983-Dec. 1983	0.97	2.61	4.79	0.38	1.55	2.52
43rd, July 1987-June 1988	2.80	4.20	4.60	3.50	4.40	6.70

Source: NSS Organisation.

is increasing day by day due to rise in population and capital intensive technology adopted inside and outside agriculture. Thus the new jobs created within agriculture and outside agriculture have failed to absorb the new entrants into labour force. More than 80 per cent of female workers are engaged in rural India. Moreover rural labourers both male and female are increasingly becoming casualised as can be seen from Table 6.4. It is clear from this table that among rural males, the proportion of casual labour increased from 338 in 1993-94 to 362 per 1000 in 1999-2000 an increase by 24 points. Among rural females, this proportion went up from 387 to 396. Thus increase in the proportion of casual labour indicates shift form secure to insecure employment. There is a pronounced declining trend in the importance of the self-employed category in both rural and urban areas.

TABLE 6.4
PROPORTION OF CASUAL LABOUR OF USUALLY EMPLOYED

	Self Employed	*Regular Employees*	*Casual Labour*
Rural Males			
1993-94	579	83	338
1999-2000	550	38	362
Rural Females			
1993-94	585	28	387
1999-2000	573	31	396

Source: NSS 55th Round (1999-2000).

Land Security

Land is an important asset and security in the event of natural hazards or life contingencies to the farmers in rural India. The pressure of population on land is continuously increasing. Though additional land has been brought under cultivation since 1961, yet per capita cultivated land has declined from 0.44 hectares in 1921 to 0.30 hectares in 1961 and further to 0.22 hectares in 1991. Most of the rural labourers don't have access to land. The NSS data show that the proportion of households who owned no land in 1982 was around 11 per cent. In 1990-91, 59.4 per cent holdings were having size of holdings less than a hectare. Small and marginal farmers together owned 78.2 per cent of holdings of size less than 2 hectares. Thus the average size of holdings in India is very small. This lack of access to land results in increase in incidence of poverty.

Food and Nutritional Security

A large number of rural poor are left out of the food security system. The Public Distribution System (PDS) in India was started with the objective of providing essential consumer goods at cheap and subsidised prices to the consumers. Many empirical studies based on the 1986-87 NSS data on PDS purchases have shown that poor were not benefiting much from PDS. The dependence of the poor on the PDS in rural area for many commodities is less than 16 per cent. This would mean that the dependence of the rural poor on the open market is much higher than on the PDS for most of the commodities. Thus the benefits to rural poor from PDS are limited. In order to make PDS more responsive to the needs of the poor, The Target Public Distribution System (TPDS) was introduced in June, 1997.

Health security and food security are interlinked. It is known that even if food is accessible, malnutrition can occur if proper hygienic conditions are not available. The NSS 43rd Round data shows that poor people spend less on health in absolute and relative terms as compared to the non-poor. With liberalisation, the cost of health maintenance is expected to increase for the poor. A health support programme is needed for the Govt. in the improvement of the health needs of the poor. In India, only small groups of people belonging to the organized sector enjoy some measure of health security in the form of health insurance.

Education Security

To increase the well being of the poor and vulnerable sections in rural areas, education is very important component of social security. Education is also important for achieving employment, food and health security. India has the largest concentration of illiterates in the world. The literacy rate was 59.40 per cent among the rural workers and 80.30 per cent for urban workers. The literacy rate for males (71.40 per cent) and females (46.7 per cent) was lower in rural areas than corresponding figures of males (86.7) and females (73.2) in urban areas in 2001. Within rural areas female workers suffer more due to lack of literacy. Thus the problem of illiteracy is much more severe among rural labourers as compared to urban labourers. Lack of education leads to greater vulnerability in the labour market. Child labour in rural areas also doesn't have security of education. Access to free and compulsory education is being shown up as the key weapon to end child labour. For a country, which is expected to be home to 50 per cent of the world's illiterate population, it is not surprising to have 78 million children between 6 and 11 years who do not go to school. According to 1991 census, about 77.70 per cent of child labour work as cultivators and agricultural labourers in India. Thus education for the rural labour seems to be a crucial parameter for the success of social security programmes in India.

Other Forms of Security

Apart from above forms of insecurity, rural labourers have little access to safe drinking water, sanitation, health care, housing etc. The provision of safe drinking water supply and sanitation facilities is a basic necessity of life and a crucial input in achieving the goal of "Health for All." According to 1991 census, percentage of population covered under rural water supply was 45 as compared to 90 in urban areas. Rural sanitation was provided to 5 per cent of population as compared to 45 per cent of population covered under urban sanitation in 1991. Rural Drinking Water Programme which has been introduced as a specific component of the new initiative for achievement of sustainable human development at the village level, launched by the Government in 2000-2001 in the form of Pradhan Mantri Gramodaya Yojana (PMGY). The Ministry of Rural Development launched the Rural Sanitation Programme in 1986 to improve the quality of life of the rural poor.

Women constitute a significant part of the workforce in the country. Amongst rural women workers, a majority (i.e. about 80 per cent in 1991 census) is employed in agriculture as labourers and cultivators. There is a pronounced declining trend in the importance of the self-employed category in rural area and an overall increase in the casualisation of the women workforce. Most of the female workers are illiterate and getting low wages. Among the rural labourers, some other vulnerable groups are old age people and widows. They suffer mainly by financial insecurity and health insecurity.

Recent Programmes

The comprehensive social security programmes are needed for rural labour in view of the prevalence of insecurity against income, employment, health, education, housing etc. Recently Government of India has adopted certain employment generation and poverty alleviation programmes, some of which are as follows:

Jawahar Gram Samridhi Yojana (JGSY)

JGSY was introduced in April 1999 by restructuring the Jawahar Rozgar Yojana. The objective of JGSY is creation of infrastructure and durable assets at the village level so as to increase opportunities for sustained employment to the rural poor. The wage employment under JGSY is provided normally to persons belonging to households below poverty line.

Sampoorna Grameen Rojgar Yojana (SGRY)

This scheme has been launched with effect from September 2001, the scheme aims at providing wage employment in rural areas as also food security, along with the creation of durable community, and social and economic assets.

Swarnjayanti Gram Swarozgar Yojana (SGSY)

SGSY was launched with effect from April 1, 1999 as a result of amalgamating certain erstwhile programmes viz. Integrated Rural Development Programme (IRDP), Development of Women and Children in Rural Areas (DWCRA), Training for Rural Youth for Self Employment (TRYSEM), Million Wells Scheme (MWS) etc. into a single self employment programme. It aims at promoting micro-enterprises and helping the rural poor into Self Help Groups (SHG).

Pradhan Mantri Gramodaya Yojana (PMGY)

PMGY was introduced in 2000-2001 with the objective of focusing on village level development in five critical areas. i.e. health, primary education, drinking water, housing and rural roads, with the overall objective of improving the quality of life of people in the rural areas.

Krishi Shramik Samajik Suraksha Yojana

This scheme was launched in July, 2001 for giving social security benefit to agricultural labourers on hire in the age group of 18 to 60 years.

Shiksha Sahayog Yojana

The scheme has been finalized for providing educational allowance of Rs. 100 per month to the children of parents living below the poverty line for their education from ninth to twelveth standard.

National Agricultural Insurance Scheme

The national agricultural insurance scheme (NAIS) was introduced in the country from the 1999-2000 Rabi season. The main objective of the scheme is to protect the farmers against losses suffered by them due to crop failure on account of natural calamities, such as, drought, flood, hail storm, cyclone, diseases etc. so as to restore their credit worthiness for the ensuing season.

How far these poverty alleviation and employment generation programmes shall be effective in providing Social Security to rural labour is yet to be seen?

Suggestions

Following are some of the important suggestions for enhancing social security of rural labour.

1. Rural labour should be provided assured income by fixing minimum wages. But fixation of minimum wages is no guarantee for their payment. Enforcement of minimum wages should become the essential component of employment programmes. Some mechanism should also be devised to link minimum

wages with the consumer price index numbers to the extent possible. Abolition of rural poverty largely depends upon the guarantee of minimum wages. According to a notification issued by the government of India in December, 1998, the Central Government has directed not to fix the minimum wages for workers in the unorganized sector below Rs. 40 per day, the basic subsistence wage. But fixation of minimum wages is no guarantee for their payment.

2. As agricultural labour has no social security, no earned leave, no sick leave and any pension or gratuity substantial efforts should be directed in this field. All the states must provide compulsory insurance and institute old age pension schemes so that the agricultural workers don't have to depend upon others in their old age.
3. The state should play the role of a regulator and facilitator. For the poorest of the poor, the state can also contribute partly to various social security schemes, which may be run by government companies, private companies and social organizations. We should strengthen all the non-state providers of social security.
4. Public Distribution System (PDS) should be linked with employment guarantee programmes. It should enable the targeting of PDS to the really needy people as persons employed on rural works programmes belong to the very poor strata of the society. Two programmes together would help in the alleviation of poverty and in meeting the minimum food requirements of the people at the same time.
5. Such programmes should be encouraged that improve the skills of the rural labourers
6. To eradicate child labour, Government laws should be implemented effectively. Primary education should be made compulsory for children in rural areas.
7. Land reforms have been recognized to constitute a vital element both in terms of the anti-poverty

strategy and for modernization and increased productivity in agriculture. Redistribution of land could provide a permanent asset base for a large number of rural landless poor for taking up land-based and other supplementary activities. Similarly, consolidation of holdings, tenancy regulation and updating of land records, would widen the access of small and marginal farmers to improved technology and input and thereby lead to increase in agricultural production. Effective implementation of land reforms is strictly required if we want to improve the lot of rural labour.

8. Government expenditure on social security programmes should be enhanced in rural areas. Both central and state governments should spend most of the resources on social sector. These resources should be effectively utilized so as to reach the poor.
9. Agricultural labourers should be provided with house sites and homesteads not only to meet their basic need but also to enable households to take up supplementary land-based activities like poultry, dairy etc.
10. There is an urgent need for a central legislation to cover agricultural labour. This legislation should provide for security of employment for agricultural labour, prescribed hours of work, etc. The legislation should also make enabling provisions to prepare schemes for welfare and social security measures.
11. Various social security and welfare schemes at the state level like old age pension, pension for agricultural landless labourers, maternity benefits, group insurance schemes for the unorganized poor and vulnerable sections of society are prevalent but the coverage is very low and limited. These schemes should be extended to all the states.
12. Unemployment insurance should be the first step to social security in rural areas.

REFERENCES

1. Bhattacharya, V.R. (1970), Some Aspects of Social Security Measures in India, Metropolitan Book Co. (Private) Ltd. New Delhi.
2. Datt, Ruddar and Sundhram, K.P.M. (2001), Indian Economy, S. Chand and Company Ltd., New Delhi.
3. Dev, S.M. (1998), "Government Interventions and social security for Rural Labour," in Radhakrishna, K. and Sharma, A.N. (Ed.) (1998), Empowering Rural Labour in India, Institute for Human Development, New Delhi.
4. Indian Economic Survey, 2001-02.
5. Misra, S.K. and Puri V.K. (2001), Indian Economy, Himalaya Publishing House, Delhi.
6. Parthasarathy, G. (1998), "Minimum Wages in Agriculture: A Review of Indian Experience," Radhakrishna, K. and Sharma, A.N. (Ed.) 1998, Empowering Rural Labour in India, Institute for Human Development, New Delhi.
7. Prasad, Eswara, K.V. (1993), Social Security for Unorganised Labour: A Review, Friedrich Ebert Stiftung, New Delhi and National labour Institute, NOIDA.
8. Rakha Krishna, K. and Sharma, A.N. (Ed.) (1998), Empowering Rural Labour in India, Institute for Human Development, New Delhi.
9. Singh, J.K. (1998), Labour Economics, Deep and Deep Publications Pvt. Ltd., New Delhi.
10. Thorat, Sukhadio, (1999), "Social Security in Unorganised Sector in India: How secure are the Scheduled Castes," Indian Journal of Labour Economics, July-Sept., Vol. 42.

7

SOCIAL SECURITY FOR WOMEN WORKERS IN INDIA

G. Subbayamma and
S. Vijaya Kumar

Introduction

"There is not a single country where women enjoy equality with men" says Human Development Report of 1995. In terms of economic contributions, Human Development Report of 1996 estimates that women perform 11 trillion dollar worth of unpaid or invisible activities world wide. Needless to say that women work longer hours than men, contribute to more than half of the wealth of the nation but receive one-tenth of the world income and own less than one per cent of the world property.

This is the scenario prevailing in many developing countries including in India. Being agrarian in characteristics, Indian society is hosting 92 per cent of the informal sector where women contribute much labour and receives less social security. They are deprived of wants and vulnerable to several forms of risks. Recognizing this fact, government of India has formulated quite a few social security schemes for women workers and this paper examines some of such schemes in nutshell.

Conventionally different economists and organizations have defined social security in different ways. Of such definitions most popular thesis of Dreze and Sen (1998) argues that using social means to prevent deprivation and vulnerability refers to social security, which has both promotional and protective measures. Through promotional measures, according to Dreze and Sen, living standards of the population can be enhanced and through protective measures basic capabilities has to be expanded.

Similarly Convention No. 102 of the International Labour Organization emphasized social insurance and social assistance is the basic forms of social security. Indian government also adopted this convention, however, gender discrimination in our patriarchal society has largely denied women right to social security measures.

Most of the social security schemes, both in the advanced as well as in the third world countries, are mainly meant for workers in the organised sector. Workers in the unorganised sector, on the other hand, are deprived of such benefits (Pillai, 1996). In the developing economies the organised sector constitutes only a small segment of the workforce while the majority belong to the unorganised sector. Workers in the unorganised sector have to often face problems of irregular employment, unstable income and absence of any legal protection in regard to income, employment and health and safety measures (Papola, 1993). It is therefore essential to provide social security for the unorganised workers from the viewpoint equity and social justice. Access to social protection is therefore considered a basic *human right,* as well as a measure of human welfare (ILO).

So far as the women workers are concerned, a still higher proportion, about 97 per cent, is concentrated in the unorganised sector. They constitute only about 12 per cent of the organised sector employment. The women's employment is mostly found to be concentrated in activities and occupations with relatively low levels of productivity, incomes and stability and security of employment. Vast sections of the economically active female population are excluded from social security programmes; more women than new lack coverage; and the absence of adequate social protection, in addition to gender discrimination in the labour market, makes women particularly vulnerable to economic deprivation, especially in the context of recent economic reforms in the country (ILO).

The following discussion mainly focused on (i) the sectoral distribution of women workers and their contribution to the economy; (ii) various forms of social insecurity of the women workers; (iii) the existing social security measures, both promotional and protective measures for women workers; (iv) the impact of structural adjustment; and (v) the need for strengthening social security schemes.

Labour Force Participation Rates for Women

Data compiled by NSS suggests that the work participation rate of women show that a considerable proportion (one-third) of the women are actively involved in economic activities thereby contributing to economic development of the country (Table 7.1) However, these women suffer from a higher incidence of unemployment than men and form about half of the total unemployed persons (Table 7.2). Here it is important to note that women's participation in economic activities has positive impact on overall development of the society including slowing down population growth, reducing poverty and child mortality (Dreze and Sen, 1995; Tulasidhar, 1993).

TABLE 7.1
WORKFORCE PARTICIPATION RATES FOR WOMEN

Year of Census NSS Survey	*Persons*	*Male*	*Female*
1911	48.2	62.0	33.9
1921	47.0	60.6	32.8
1931	43.6	57.9	28.4
1951	39.1	53.9	23.4
1961	43.0	57.1	28.0
1971	34.0	52.7	13.9
1972-73 NSS	40.7	52.7	27.8
1977-78 NSS	41.8	53.5	29.3
1991	37.5	51.6	22.3
1993-94 NSS	42.0	54.5	28.6

Source: Visaria, op.cit. (1996).

TABLE 7.2
UNEMPLOYMENT RATES BY SEX, RESIDENCE AND STATUS

Sector/	1972-73			1977-78			1983			1987-88		
Status	M	F	T	M	F	T	M	F	T	M	F	T
Rural												
UPS	–	–	–	2.22	5.52	3.26	2.12	1.14	1.91	2.87	3.52	3.07
UPSS	1.16	0.48	0.92	1.28	2.01	1.54	1.41	0.66	1.13	1.81	2.27	1.98
CWS	3.02	5.51	3.86	3.57	4.13	3.74	3.72	4.26	3.88	4.16	4.27	4.19
CDS	6.83	11.22	8.21	7.12	9.18	7.70	7.52	8.98	7.94	4.58	6.91	5.25
Urban												
UPS	–	–	–	2.22	5.52	3.26	2.12	1.41	1.91	2.87	3.52	3.07
UPSS	1.16	0.48	0.92	1.28	2.01	1.54	1.41	0.66	1.13	1.81	2.27	1.98
CWS	3.02	5.51	3.86	3.57	4.13	3.74	3.72	4.26	3.38	4.16	4.27	4.19
Total												
UPS	–	–	–	3.07	7.01	4.23	3.02	2.14	2.77	3.60	4.19	3.77
UPSS	1.90	1.02	1.61	2.79	3.19	2.47	2.28	1.16	1.90	2.56	2.72	2.62
CWS	3.61	5.87	4.32	4.29	4.97	4.48	4.44	4.70	4.51	4.75	4.92	4.80
CDS	7.07	11.46	8.35	7.59	9.86	8.18	7.93	9.26	8.28	5.54	7.61	6.09

* Unemployed as percentage of labour force.
UP: Usual Principal Status;
CWS: Current Weekly Status;
UPSS: Usual Principal and Subsidiary Status;
CDS: Current Daily Status.
M—Male, F—Female, T—Total.

Wage discrimination is another major concern for women workers. As per the data provided by NSS reveal that gender based wage differentials exist in almost all sector of the economy. Women get less wages than their male counterparts even for the equal nature and amount of work being performed by them (Table 7.3).

It is therefore necessary to ensure greater productive employment for women by introducing government programmes, which can also reduce discrimination in wage payment for women.

Various Forms of Insecurity for Women Workers

There are several forms of insecurity making women workers more vulnerable to multiple risks and thereby

TABLE 7.3
AVERAGE WAGE/SALARY EARNINGS PER DAY RECEIVED BY REGULAR WAGE/SALARIED EMPLOYEES OF AGE GROUP 15-59 YEARS BY INDUSTRY/SECTOR, IN INDIA DURING 1987-88

	Average Wage per day					
	Rural			*Urban*		
Industry	*Male*	*Female*	*Difference (Rs.)*	*Male*	*Female*	*Difference (Rs.)*
Agriculture, Hunting & Forestry	14.58	10.65	3.93	27.57	19.05	8.52
Fishing	38.70	23.81	14.89	46.28	31.37	14.55
Mining & Quarrying	22.77	9.42	13.35	29.83	13.06	16.77
Manufacturing	28.69	13.78	14.91	43.49	33.20	10.39
Electricity, Gas & Water	36.16	45.17	–9.01	50.14	43.92	33.20
Construction	36.16	45.17	–9.01	50.14	43.92	6.22
Wholesale & Retail Trade & Restaurant Hotels	31.58	18.27	13.31	39.23	27.65	11.58
Transport, Storage & Communication Services	17.99	18.42	–0.43	22.55	18.37	4.18
Financial Insurance, Real Estate & Business services	46.25	38.75	7.50	62.10	53.92	8.18
Community Social and Personal Services	38.54	28.39	10.15	46.51	36.33	10.18

Source: Sarvekshana (Special Number) NSSO, Government of India.

weakening their risk absorption and management capacities. Some of the forms of insecurity are discussed hereunder.

Poverty

The incidence of poverty has increased significantly during the recent period. Rural labour are the worst affected since the increase in poverty is much higher in rural areas. About 65% of the total workforce in the country is confined to the agriculture sector. But of the total women workers 82 per cent are in this sector (Papola, 1991). Further, there has been a significant growth of female-headed households. Households maintained by women alone, and especially those with young children are more vulnerable to poverty.

Uncertainty of Employment

A vast majority of women workers are in the unorganised sector, engaged predominantly as agricultural labourers or as home-based workers. The main characteristics of these workers are that they have no regular continued employment under a particular employer for a long period. This leads to highly uncertain employment for women workers.

Unstable Income

Most of the poor women have only their physical labour to sell. In the absence of regular employment or any other sources of income, these women workers suffer from high-income insecurity and uncertainty. Further, evidence shows stagnation in real wages during the last decade. Due to segmentation in the labour market, women workers cannot move out easily from areas of low wages to areas of high wages.

Casualisation

The uncertainty of employment for women has been increasing as more and more women workers are becoming casualised. The share of female casual workers in the female workers increased from 23.3 per cent in 1972/73 to 29.9 per cent in 1987/88. This casualisation effect is, however, higher in rural areas which increased from 31.4 per cent to 35.4 per cent during the period. In urban areas, their proportion increased from 23.7 per cent to 25.4 per cent. It may also be noted that the proportion of casual workers has remained higher among female than among male workers (Table 7.4).

TABLE 7.4
PERCENTAGE DISTRIBUTION OF WORKERS BY CATEGORY OF EMPLOYMENT

	Rural			*Urban*			
	Males	*Females*	*Total*	*Males*	*Female*	*Total*	*Combined (Rural+Urban)*
Self Employment							
1972-73	65.3	64.5	65.4	39.2	48.4	40.9	61.4
1977-78	62.8	62.1	62.5	40.4	49.5	42.4	59.3
1983	62.4	61.9	61.0	40.9	45.8	41.9	57.3
1987-88	68.8	60.9	59.4	41.6	47.1	42.8	56.3
Salaried regular employment							
1972-73	12.1	4.1	9.2	50.7	27.8	46.5	15.3
1977-78	11.8	2.8	7.8	46.4	24.9	41.7	13.2
1983	10.8	2.8	7.5	43.7	25.8	39.9	13.7
1987-88	10.6	3.6	7.7	43.4	27.5	40.2	13.7
Casual wage employment							
1972-73	2.0	31.4	25.4	10.1	23.7	12.8	23.3
1977-78	26.7	35.1	29.7	13.2	25.6	15.9	27.5
1983	20.2	35.3	31.5	15.4	28.4	18.2	28.9
1987-88	31.4	35.4	32.8	14.7	25.4	17.0	29.9

Source: Centre for Monitoring Indian Economy (CMIE), 1991.

A large number of women employed as casual labourers in construction and other industries do not get the prescribed minimum wages, nor are the stipulated minimum hours of work adhered to. The traditional economic activities, which provide employment to women, have suffered in competition with the more advanced technologies (Eighth Five Year Plan).

Segmentation of Labour Market

It has been generally observed that women are subjected to labour market discrimination and are relegated to low paying and low status works; they are pushed to the periphery in employment causing 'feminisation' of occupations. Women have been marginalised in the process of development; they are mostly excluded from productive work; pushed into and continued in marginal occupations and are increasingly casualised in terms of employment

(Varghese, 1991). Wage rates and earnings are lower for women than for men and the position of women remains inferior, even in the unorganised sector.

Access to Land/Common Property Resources

Though women constitute most of the breadwinners in rural areas, majority of these women do not have access to land. The extent and quality of access of rural poor to common land have also deteriorated in recent years. The agricultural labourers derived their major part of fuel and fodder supply from common lands. The common lands made significant contribution to their employment and income. The diminishing access to common property adversely affects the rural poor and particularly the women labourers (Jodha, 1986).

Illiteracy

Data indicate that the illiteracy among the female workers is quite high both in rural (82.2 per cent) as well as urban (55.1 per cent) areas (Table 7.5). High illiteracy among women would result in their low quality of employment, which is characterised by low incomes and without stability, and security of employment.

TABLE 7.5
ILLITERACY OF THE USUAL STATUS WORKERS (ABOVE 15 YEARS): ALL INDIA, RURAL AND URBAN; 1987-88

Sex	*Rural*	*Urban*
Male (%)	48.9	20.3
Female (%)	82.9	55.1

Source: Sarvekshana, Special Issue on 43rd Round on Employment and Unemployment, All India, 1990.

Apart from the above, the other forms of insecurity include access to health and maternity care, food security, and old age.

Social Security Measures

The Government's approach towards achieving poverty

alleviation and social security takes two forms: (a) growth-oriented promotional policies, and (b) direct intervention in anti-poverty and social security programmes. This section briefly evaluates the promotional and protective measures of social security by the Government through direct interventions. Special efforts have been made to improve women's access to asset and employment under various programmes.

Promotional Social Security Measures, which include—

(i) Wage employment programmes—Jawahar Rojgar Yojana (JRY).

(ii) Self employment programmes—Integrated Rural Development Programme (IRDP).

(iii) Provision of basic needs on subsidised basis, for example, primary education, basic health services, etc.

(iv) Public distribution system (PDS) and nutrition programmes like Integrated Child Development Services (ICDS).

Protective Social Security Measures include schemes at state level to provide financial assistance against contingencies such as sickness, old age, maternity etc.

Promotional Social Security Measures

Jawahar Rojgar Yojana (JRY)

It was initiated in 1989-90, which is implemented in all the villages. The programme continues to be the largest single anti-poverty programme, with the primary objective of generating additional gainful employment for the unemployed persons in the rural areas. People below the poverty line constitute the target group and at least 30 per cent of the employment opportunities are earmarked for women. Five per cent of the total funds allocated to JRY subject to a maximum of Rs. 75 crores are to be kept apart for taking up special projects aimed at prevention of migration of labourers, enhancing women's employment and special programmes through voluntary organizations.

A quick evaluation of the JRY conducted by the Programme Evaluation Organisation of the Planing Commission reveals that on an average 15-25 days of employment were provided to each beneficiary and is far below the JRY target of 50 man-days of employment per poor household. The share of women also has been only 20 per cent despite the 30 per cent earmarking for them on JRY works.

Employment Assurance Scheme (EAS)

This new scheme was introduced in 1993 in identified backward blocks with the objective of providing assured employment up to 100 days to rural adults—men and women—who are seeking wage employment and willing to do manual work. The other objective is the creation of economic infrastructure and community assets of sustained employment and development. As on March 1996, the total number of blocks covered under EAS are 3,197 and the number of people registered are over 20 million. During 1995/96 a total of 333.87 million person days' employment was generated. The share of women was 29 per cent during the period.

Integrated Rural Development Programme (IRDP)

This is one of the most important anti-poverty programmes in the country. Introduced during the Sixth Five Year Plan (1980-85), it is a subsidized credit programme providing access to low interest bank credit to rural beneficiaries for acquisition of productive assets or appropriate skills of self-employment. To ensure better participation of women in the development process it has been decided that at lest 30 per cent of those assisted should be women. The target for women was even raised from 30 per cent to 40 per cent in 1990-91. Data show that the coverage of women has been constantly rising under IRDP from 10 per cent in 1985-86 to 34 per cent in 1995-96 (Table 7.6).

Studies however indicate that the programme suffers from various shortcomings: those who are not eligible enjoy substantial part of the benefits; proportion of women and SC/STs assisted falls short of targets, assets obtained under the programme are inappropriate.

TABLE 7.6
COVERAGE OF WOMEN UNDER IRDP
(PERCENTAGE TO TOTAL COVERAGE), 1985-86 to 1994-95

Year	*1985-86*	*1986-87*	*1987-88*	*1988-89*	*1989-90*	*1990-91*	*1991-92*	*1992-93*	*1993-94*	*1994-95*
%	9.90	15.13	19.54	23.17	25.63	30.88	33.15	33.39	33.62	33.90

Source: Government of India (1996).

Training of Rural Youth for Self Employment (TRYSEM)

This is centrally sponsored scheme introduced on August 1979. TRYSEM aims at providing technical and entrepreneurial skills to rural youth from families below poverty line to enable them taking up income generating activities. Under TRYSEM, technical skills are imparted to rural in the age group 18-35 at selected training instituted. The coverage given for women is 40 per cent. The percentage of women trained under the programme increased from 34 during the Sixth Plan to 50 by the Eight Plan period.

Development of Women and Children in Rural Areas (DWCRA)

First started as pilot project in 50 districts during 1982-83, with UNICEF cooperation (withdrawn from January 1996), has now been extended to all districts in the country. It was mainly intended to improve women's participation in rural development and to strengthen the women's component of Poverty Alleviation Programme. Selection of districts is made on the basis of low female literacy, high infant mortality rate so that the most backward section of the rural population could derive the benefits first.

The women members of DWCRA form into groups of 10-15 women each for taking up economic activities suited to their skill and local conditions. A revolving fund of

Rs. 25,000 (to be shared by the central and state governments) is given to each group to meet their working capital requirements. Support for marketing of products of the women's groups is being encouraged. NGOs have been involved in the implementation of the programme since its inception. An assessment of DWCRA reveals considerable progress in the programme in recent years (Table 7.7).

TABLE 7.7
ACHIEVEMENTS UNDER DWCRA SINCE INCEPTION

Plans	*Target (No. of Groups)*	*Achievement (No. of Groups)*	*No. of Women Benefited*	*Utilization of funds (Rs. in lakhs)*
VI Plan	6035	3308	52170	298.53
VII Plan	35000	28031	469707	3663.53
1990-91	7500	7139	109557	898.00
1991-92	7500	8043	141132	962.72
VIII Plan	61900	83668	1451149	11209.73
Grand Total	117935	130189	2223715	16425.22

Source: Government of India (1996 a).

The problems of DWCRA are as follows: through a number of groups have been formed under DWCRA only some of them started economic activities; marketing of products poses a major problem; most groups took up traditional economic activities and did not go for non-traditional activities (Hirway and Unni, 1992).

Despite the problems, the DWCRA model seems to be the best one among all the State interventions for increasing women's employment because DWCRA is the only programme of its kind which aims at empowering the rural poor women through economic means (Dev, 1996).

Maharashtra Employment Guarantee Scheme (EGS)

Introduced in 1972, with the primary objective of providing guarantee of work to all those who live in rural areas and who are prepared to do unskilled manual labour, the scheme covers all adults. The data show that there has been a gradual increase in the percentage of women participating in the EGS. The proportion of women increased from 41.4 per cent in 1979 to 53.3 per cent in 1987. However, there have been fluctuations in the proportion of women's participation.

Barring some limitations, the EGS has made positive impact on the levels of living of women in the state. There has been a considerable decline in the unemployment rate for females and their incomes have increased.

Protective Social Security Measures

Several state governments initiated various protective social security measures for the vulnerable sections in the unorganised sector. A review of these schemes reveal that: almost all states and union territories have old age pension schemes; some states have special pension schemes for destitute widows and the physically handicapped; maternity benefits for landless agricultural labour have been introduced in some states, unemployment relief schemes exist in some, while certain welfare schemes exclusively for women and children have been introduced by some states. However, the coverage under these schemes is not high.

After examining the impact of social security schemes for unorganised labour, Prasad (1993) arrives at the following conclusions: (a) the quantum of assistance given to the beneficiaries were negligibly low; (b) women are the most neglected in the implementation of the schemes; (c) the coverage has been very poor for women even with respect to specific schemes meant for them; (d) the procedures to apply and obtaining the assistance is so complicated for women. Another study by Prasad (1995) reveals that the widow's scheme in Dindigul district is hardly accessible to widows with its rigid procedures and insensitivity to the needs of these widows.

NGOs and Women Development

One of the most important programmes of social security for women is the integrated work security insurance scheme being implemented by Self Employed Women's

Association (SEWA). It brought together poor self-employed women in the unorganised sector and is striving to get them a fair deal in various economic activities. SEWA has evolved a maternity benefit scheme, and also runs creches for children of its members in rural and urban areas.

Another grassroot organisation for the upliftment of women workers is the Working Women Forum (WWF) operating in South India. The organisation has achieved a good deal of success in the spheres of education, health, nutrition and family welfare.

Impact of Structural Adjustment on Women Workers

The recent structural adjustment measures or the transition from socialist to market economies have led to sudden reductions in real incomes of the poor. This has adverse impact on women workers majority of who are in the unorganised sector. Even in the organised sector, due to the ongoing process of structural reform and privatization of industries, women workers are deprived of job security, maternity benefits, etc. There is a growing tendency towards employment of casual/contract labourers as a result of which women have no regularity or security of employment.

To cite an example, illegal retrenchment, voluntary retirement schemes initiated in the private and public sector which have wiped out a whole generation of middle aged and older women workers in the pharmaceutical, soaps and cosmetics and electronics industries, i.e., in the age group of 40 years and above (Chhachi, et.al. 1996).

Standing (1991) points out that to assess the effects of structural adjustment on employment and conditions of employment, it is important to distinguish between various type of worker security to which protective regulations apply.

Enhancing the Social Security of Women Workers

Issues that need to be considered here are—

1. Implementation of minimum wages is one of the important means of social security for women

workers, which would also reduce the wage discrimination to a large extent.

2. The employment generation programmes and poverty alleviation programmes should be implemented in the true sense, which would bring the women into the mainstream.
3. Investment in public works programmes which have higher employment growth potentiality. This would bring about the desired social transformation and the objective of providing continuous employment for women.
4. Self-help groups often represent an important means of guaranteeing a minimum of social and economic security in the informal sections of the society. The State should provide support to these organizations/ groups.
5. Public expenditure on social security programmes should be increased in the poorer states where the coverage is inadequate.
6. The administrative aspects in implementing the existing social security schemes should be simplified so that they are accessible to the poor women.

Concluding Observations

It is necessary to identify various insecurities for which the women workers are more vulnerable than men. These include: poverty, uncertainty of employment, unstable income, casualisation, segmentation of labour market, illiteracy, little access to land, etc.

The approach towards social security includes; (1) Promotional measures-wage employment programmes, self-employment programmes, provision of healthcare, education, public distribution system and (2) Protective schemes at the state level. The assessment of the above programmes reveals that the coverage is inadequate. Also, there is considerable variation between the earmarking for different purposes, different target groups and for wage employment in the JRY on one hand and what obtains in reality on the other hand.

One cannot escape the conclusion that the centre's anti-poverty portfolio is riddled with much needless confusion and complexity in its conceptualisation, design and administration (Guhan, 1995). A comprehensive social security programme may be introduced at the national level. The decentralised operation of such a programme with the help of NGOs would immensely help the poor women workers.

REFERENCES

Chhachi, A et.al (1996), "Revisiting Casualisation, Flexibility and Feminization: Implications for women workers' lives", Paper presented at the Seminar on Gender and Employment in India—Recent Trends, Patterns and Policy Options, December 18-20, New Delhi.

Dev, Mahendra S. (1996), "State Interventions and Women's Employment", Paper presented at the Seminar on Gender and Employment in India—Recent Trends, Patterns and Policy Options, December 18-20, New Delhi.

Dreze, Jean and Sen A. (1998), *Hunger and Public Action,* Clarendon Press, Oxford.

Guhan, S (1995), Social Expenditures in the Union Budget, *Economic and Political Weekly,* Vol. 30, No. 18 and 19.

Hirway, Indira and Unni, Jemol (1992), "Women in Industry and Technology: Two Successful Studies", in Sharma, A.N. and Seema Singh (eds.), *Women and work, changing scenario in India,* Indian Society of Labour Economics and B.R. Publishing Corporation, Delhi.

International Labour Organisation, (1994), Promotion of Equality and Opportunity and Treatment for Women Workers An ILO Manual for Asia and the Pacific, ILO EASMA, Bangkok.

Jodha, N.S. (1986), Common Property Resources and Rural Poor in Dry Regions of India, *Economic and Political Weekly,* Vol. 21, No. 27.

Papola T.S. (1991), "Recent Changes in the Structure of Women's Employment," Paper Presented at Planning Commission—World Bank Workshop on Gender and Poverty in India, December 5-7, New Delhi.

Papola T.S. (1993), "Employment of Women in South Asian Countries", *Indian Journal of Labour Economics,* Vol. 36, No. 1.

Pillai, M. (1996), 'Social Security for workers in Unorganised Sector-Experience of Kerala', *Economic and Political Weekly,* August 3.

Prasad Eswara, K.V. (1993), *Social Security for Unorganised Labour: A*

Review, Friedrich Ebert Stiftuing, New Delhi and National Labour Institute, NOIDA (Mimeo).

Prasad Eswara, K.V. (1995), "Social Security for Destitute Widows in Tamil Nadu", *Economic and Political Weekly,* Vol. 30, No. 15.

Som, B.M. (1994), *'Towards Developing a Social Security System for the Agricultural Sector',* Social Security Association of India, New Delhi.

Standing, Guy (1991), *Structural Adjustment and Labour Market Policies Towards Social Adjustment.*

Tulasidhar, V.B. (1993), 'Maternal Education, Female Labour Force Participation and Child Mortality: Evidence from Indian Census,' *Health Transition Review,* Vol. 3, No. 2.

Varghese, N.V. (1991), 'Women and work: An Examination of the Female Marginalisatioin Thesis', *Indian Journal of Labour Economics,* Vol. 34, No. 3.

Visaria, Pravin (1996), 'Level and Pattern of Female Employment in India, 1911-1994', Paper Presented at Seminar on "Gender and Employment in India—Recent Trends, Patterns and Policy Options', December 18-20, New Delhi.